DELIVER US FROM EVIL

DELIVER US
FROM EVIL

DON BASHAM

chosen for you chosen books

Washington Depot, Connecticut 06794

Distributed by Fleming H. Revell Company
Old Tappan, New Jersey

ISBN 0-912376-06-6

Library of Congress Catalog Card Number: 72-81891
Printed in the United States of America

A Note about the Delicate Matter of Names

ANY book dealing with a minister's relationship to people faces a dual problem. On the one hand, he must tell the truth exactly as it happened, without concealing or altering the facts. On the other, he has a pastoral obligation to protect the confidence of those whom he serves.

I have solved this dilemma in the usual not-altogether-satisfactory way: where relating a story might cause harm or embarrassment, I have changed names, and occasionally locale or other external circumstances that might permit identification.

In every other respect, these events are recounted exactly as I experienced them.

Don Basham
Pompano Beach, Florida

DELIVER US FROM EVIL

1

The Move

IT COULDN'T be God's will for us to come to a place like this!" I complained to my wife, Alice, as we drove up the unfamiliar street leading out of town.

An invitation from the pulpit committee of the East Side Church had brought us the 350 miles from Toronto, Canada, to visit the small mill town of Sharon, Pennsylvania. The weekend had been pleasant enough, insofar as the East Side people were concerned. But the contrast between the broad clean streets of Toronto and the drab business section of Sharon seemed only to symbolize the intangible differences between the two places.

The fact was, we were in the midst of a spiritual revival in our Hillcrest Church in Toronto and no minister wants to leave a church where God is performing miracles. At least I didn't, and apparently Alice felt the same way.

"I know what you mean," she said. "After what's been happening in Hillcrest this church seems so—well, complacent."

That was it exactly. The Sharon congregation had precisely the kind of tame, unexpectant, it's-Sunday-so-it's-time-for-church approach that the Toronto church had had before a number of us

became involved in what is known as the "charismatic renewal."
Now all preconceived notions and self-sufficiency were swept aside
as week after week we witnessed the supernatural manifestations
of the Holy Spirit. Among other things there had been remarkable
cases of healing in response to prayer.

One of the first of these had occurred when a young woman
came to our midweek prayer meeting on crutches and in great
pain. Suffering from severely impaired circulation in one leg—
a condition which had previously put her in the hospital for many
months and left her partially paralyzed—she had finally recovered, only to have the condition recur, putting her back on
crutches. The leg was numb and useless, yet even to touch that
foot to the floor brought excruciating pain.

We gathered round her. Even as we prayed, circulation began
to improve: before the meeting ended she had discarded one
crutch and was gingerly putting weight on the bad leg. Next morning she telephoned to report she had discarded the other crutch
and was completely healed. The experience had greatly stirred the
congregation.

Besides miracles of healing there had been experiences of
prophetic dreams and visions. A number of people attending the
meetings had entered into the spiritual experience known as the
baptism in the Holy Spirit, first described in the New Testament
on the day of Pentecost, and usually accompanied by the phe-
nomenon called "speaking in tongues."

I was most grateful for all that was happening. For a long
time I had preached that the Christian life offered joy and victory and wholeness; here were living illustrations of the truth I
believed in.

It was no wonder, then, that the prospect of leaving Hillcrest
Church did not excite us. We had responded to the invitation to
visit Sharon only out of courtesy. Why the East Side congregation had singled me out, we had no idea. But both Alice and I

had been struck by the timing of the letter from them. When we had left a pastorate in Washington, D.C., to move to Toronto in 1961, we had planned to spend three years in Canada. Now it was 1964, and here came the letter.

On the long drive back to Toronto, Alice and I continued to discuss it. East Side was not without interesting aspects. It was a "federated congregation," formerly two separate churches—Baptist and Disciples of Christ—which had united with the agreement that they would alternate denominations in choosing a pastor. Their last minister had been Baptist; I was ordained in the Disciples Church. That part intrigued us, along with the timing. But—how could we tear ourselves away from Hillcrest!

Neither of us realized that the visit to Sharon was prelude to a series of events which would totally alter the course of our lives. Nor that among those events would be failures quite the opposite of the victories we were currently experiencing. Failures including the friend whose difficulty would defy our ministry and eventually cost her her life.

It was long after midnight when we arrived back at the parsonage in Toronto. After taking our babysitter home, I locked the door and carried the suitcases upstairs. In the hallway, I took Alice by the hand.

"Want to take inventory with me?"

"I already have," she smiled. "But I'll be happy to do it again." Together we went from room to room, looking in on our five sleeping children. The first was Cindi; thirteen, snuggled deep under the covers until only the tip of a pert nose peeked through the mass of blonde hair. Cindi was a regular attender at the midweek prayer meetings.

In the next bedroom lay Sharon, our elfin, brown-eyed eight-year-old. "Hi, Daddy," she mumbled sleepily as I bent to kiss her.

In the bed opposite her lay three-year-old Lisa, our second blue-eyed blonde. Alice squeezed my hands as we gazed at her, and

I knew she was remembering how a few short months before, Lisa had been instantly healed of violent stomach cramps during one of our prayer meetings. Apparently God's touch had been more than physical, for since that time she had spoken about Jesus as matter-of-factly as about playmates she could see and touch. We couldn't understand it, but we rejoiced in it.

In the small bedroom behind the bathroom slept six-year-old Glenn, looking, as he slept, like a brown-haired angel. Only the toy rockets, airplanes, and football helmet through which we threaded our way to the bedside recalled the small cyclone who inhabited our house in the daytime.

Finally, there was baby Laura, our six-month-old "Canadian" and third blue-eyed blonde, asleep in her crib in the corner of our bedroom. To look at her was to see both Cindi and Lisa as babies, the resemblance between the three was so strong.

Together, Alice and I thanked God for the five precious lives He had entrusted to our care and, minutes later, we were ourselves fast asleep.

"You know, we really got along very well without you and Alice over the weekend." It was Earl Corbett, chairman of our church board who made the half-teasing comment to me next morning as he dropped by my office at the church. Earl and his wife, Irene, had been the first in Hillcrest to receive the baptism in the Holy Spirit, followed within days by a remarkable healing. Earl's right eye, which had been crossed and half-closed since birth, was miraculously restored through prayer. The combined experiences had transformed him from a shy retiring church member into a vital, witnessing Christian.

But with Earl's wife things were different. Quietly devoted to her husband and deeply interested in the new spiritual life swirling around her, Irene had not seemed able to enter fully into the blessings which were accruing to others. Although happier and more emotionally secure than she had been in the past, she still suffered from a physical problem which had plagued her since childhood.

Irene was an epileptic.

Competent medical care enabled her to function normally much of the time; nevertheless we were puzzled by the seeming impotence of prayer in her behalf. Why, I wondered, had God granted Earl such a marvelous miracle of healing while Irene's condition remained unchanged?

Even more strange to us at the time (although I was later to glimpse the sinister significance of it) was the timing of Irene's seizures. They generally seemed to occur either during the Sunday morning worship service or at the Wednesday prayer meeting.

Two weeks after our return from Sharon, we were midway through a midweek meeting when Irene began to manifest the symptoms of epileptic seizure.

"Let's pray for Irene," Alice suggested. Earl, sitting next to his wife, put his arm around her protectively as we united in prayer. Suddenly the strange, animal-like chattering noises we had come to associate with Irene's disease began to pour from her lips. Her body trembled violently and she slumped over against Earl. After a few moments she grew quiet and the trembling ceased. She sat up and for an instant I thought our prayers had brought her through to a quick recovery. Then I saw the angry glare in her eyes, like that of a caged animal. It was an expression I was to see numerous times on the faces of people I would be ministering to in the years ahead.

"Where am I?" Irene wailed. "What place is this?" She began fumbling desperately to open the purse on her lap.

"You're with me, Irene," Earl tried to reassure her. "And we're in the prayer meeting at the church." And he reached to help her open her purse.

"Leave me alone!" Irene retorted sharply, giving his hand a

resounding slap. "Who are you? I don't know you!" And she rose to her feet unsteadily and lurched toward the door. Halfway across the room Earl caught her and looked imploringly at me.

"I haven't seen her this bad before. Can someone take us home?"

"I'll take you, Earl," I replied, my own concern for Irene mingled suddenly with a strange, smothering fear I found hard to put down. "The rest of you pray!" Earl and I ushered Irene out the door, and wedged her between us in the front seat of my car. As I backed from the church parking lot and headed in the direction of their apartment, Irene continued to struggle.

"Who are you?" she screamed at Earl. "Let me out of this car!" and she lunged for the door, fumbling for the handle as she tried to crawl over Earl.

"Irene, listen to me! It's Earl, your husband! We're taking you home! Don't you understand?"

At his words, I felt Irene go limp beside me. "Husband? Home? I don't have a husband and I don't have a home!" Earl had taken out his handkerchief and was wiping her lips and chin.

I pulled up in front of their apartment. "Would you pray once more before we go in?" Earl asked. I nodded, my own heart pounding. What was this formless fear churning within me? It did not seem directly connected with Irene's epilepsy; it was some haunting, forgotten terror of my own.

Following the prayer, Irene seemed calmer. "I'll take her inside now," Earl said, and like a docile child Irene followed him out of the car.

"Let me know if you need any more help," I called after them and was relieved to hear Irene's own natural voice respond:

"Thank you, Reverend Basham. Goodnight."

Back at church I assured the people that Irene was better. Later, at home, I told Alice about Irene's continued strange behavior in the car.

"I just can't understand it!" I concluded. "Why, with all the other answers to prayer, can't she get lasting help?"

Alice nodded sympathetically. "I know, sweetheart. I've wondered about it too. But you know, tonight Irene's behavior made me wonder if her problem isn't something more than . . ." She didn't finish the sentence.

"More than what?"

"More than just a physical problem."

"What do you mean?"

"I'm not sure," she said slowly. "But—Don that just wasn't Irene! For a minute there I could actually imagine I saw someone else looking out of her eyes!"

"What are you trying to say?"

"I don't know." Alice lifted her hands hopelessly. "I just know I saw something evil, something that wasn't any part of the Irene I know."

"Now let's be sensible," I scolded her. "I admit her behavior was plenty bizarre, but personality change is probably one of the symptoms of this disease." I was determined to keep what had happened in some familiar context.

Sure enough, the next morning Earl telephoned to say that Irene had slept well during the night and aside from feeling a little tired, seemed perfectly all right. And our concern over the incident soon faded into the background behind a more personal matter.

Although Alice and I had agreed on the drive home from Sharon, Pennsylvania, that we had no desire to change pastorates, I had neglected to write the Sharon pulpit committee of our decision. A few days after the episode with Irene, I received a letter from the Sharon church. At a congregational meeting they had voted to extend us the call to be their minister.

As Alice and I prayed over the matter, Earl's words kept coming back to me. "We really got along very well without you."

Perhaps this truly was God's moment for a move—just because things *were* going so well here. Perhaps when His Holy Spirit took over it was time for the minister to step aside, to stand down, to seek a place and a people where His fire had not yet fallen.

We wrote the East Side pulpit committee that we would come.

2

Appointment at Noon

WE BEGAN our ministry in Sharon in September of 1964 and the first months at East Side Church flew swiftly by as we slipped into the various routines connected with any new pastorate. Getting settled in the parsonage, enrolling the older children in school, meeting with church committees, systematic visitation of the membership, plus the prayerful planning of first goals.

From the beginning of my ministry in Sharon I emphasized the importance of the life of prayer. In addition I made casual but repeated reference to the charismatic renewal in Christianity, making plain my own support of this vital move. My preaching was something of a contrast to the previous ministry, but by the end of our first year I felt that my approach was well accepted.

Beginning our second year in Sharon, I also assumed the task of teaching a large adult Sunday school class, as well as conducting a Sunday evening Bible study. Out of that Bible study the first spiritual breakthrough occurred.

Alice and I had been anticipating the time when we could begin a prayer meeting. Yet experience had taught us that such a thing must grow out of genuine spiritual hunger: a vital prayer meeting is not simply something you announce or organize.

So we were delighted when the months of consistent Bible teaching produced that hunger. One Sunday night several parishioners approached me. "Why don't we begin a midweek prayer meeting? Not the ordinary kind we had years ago, but a time of real openness where we seek the kind of answers the Bible talks about."

So our Wednesday evening prayer meetings were born and almost immediately things started to happen. Remarkable answers to prayer occurred, just as they had in Toronto. One woman who came to her first meeting with some nervousness returned the following week to testify with tears in her eyes how a heart palpitation she had suffered for years had simply disappeared as she sat worshiping with us. And her healing proved permanent.

Others who sought the power of Jesus for healing came to realize they had never really known Jesus himself; at least not in a personal way. As one amazed deacon commented, "I've been a member of this church for twenty-seven years and until tonight I never knew an actual relationship with my Lord was possible."

Among the encouragements during our first year and a half in Sharon were periodic visits by members of Hillcrest Church, Toronto. On two occasions Earl and Irene Corbett spent the weekend with us in our home. We were delighted to hear that the prayer meetings in Toronto were still going strong.

"And we're still believing for Irene's healing," Earl announced cheerfully on the first visit. Irene was her usual quiet self, but so far as we could tell, there had been no real change in her condition. The epileptic seizures had grown neither more frequent nor less.

On their second visit Earl spoke at our Sunday evening Bible study; people were deeply moved by his testimony to the healing of his eye, and his matter-of-fact account of other miracles in the Toronto prayer meetings. Some of the stories I had previously shared from the pulpit, but somehow they seemed more authentic coming from a layman.

Also, during their second visit, Earl seemed jubilant about Irene. "Her healing is almost complete," he told us. "She's had lots fewer seizures lately. Even the doctors see a difference—they've let her cut down on her medicine."

And there was a change in Irene; a kind of inner glow about her. "God has been so good to me," she said. "To think that after all these years I'm really getting better!"

This was an altogether different person from the woman who had struggled so wildly in my car two years before. Why then did I feel a cold little shudder of premonition as they drove away from the parsonage on Monday morning?

"See you again in a few months," Earl called as they backed out the driveway. "And we'll have even more to tell then."

But the next report we would hear concerning the Corbetts would be of a vastly different kind, and would come with a devastating effect on my own ministry.

It is common knowledge among clergymen that the first year or so in a new parish is like a honeymoon. Both minister and congregation are on their good behavior. The minister doesn't know his people well enough to share deeply in their problems, and the congregation tends to view their minister in terms of what they hope he will be instead of what he really is—a man with struggles and weaknesses of his own.

It was midway during our second year in Sharon that things began to go wrong. Not big things, at first, just the kind of disconcerting squabbles that strain tempers and relationships in any parish. One had to do with the physical plant. Some years previously, East Side had erected a new sanctuary and at the time I arrived was using the old church building to house the Sunday school. But there were problems with it: termites, a leaking roof, rotting floorboards. Most of the younger families in the church felt that we would save money in the long run by tearing the old structure down and erecting a new educational wing. The older folks, though, those who had worshiped in "that sacred old building" since childhood, were fiercely determined to preserve it.

It was the kind of conflict that arises in every church; at such times in previous parishes I had been able to act as moderator between factions without taking sides myself. After all, the congregation would decide the issue, not me.

In Sharon, however, it appeared that I was not going to be permitted this nonaligned role. "If you don't cast your vote to save the old church," one elderly man told me, "you're no pastor of mine."

In the end, the vote went against the old building, and I set out to visit those whose sense of loss would be keenest. Gradually, most became reconciled to the majority decision. But some did not—and these seemed to hold me personally responsible. The elderly man I mentioned had often told me how much my weekly visit meant; it was one of the few events in a very restricted life. From the day of the vote on, he was never home to my knock. I would spot him sitting on his porch as my car rounded the corner: by the time I reached his front steps the porch would be empty, only the rocking chair moving rhythmically back and forth on the creaking boards . . .

Indeed, it soon began to seem to me that whatever I did, there would be hard feelings somewhere. I had written an article for *Christian Life* magazine about our Wednesday night meetings. When the editor of the magazine, Bob Walker, phoned me from a nearby town one Saturday I asked him, on impulse, to speak at our worship service the following morning. He graciously agreed and his talk was both inspiring and, I knew from later comments, helpful.

Other comments, however, were less positive. It was not Bob's sermon anyone objected to, but my having asked him without advising the proper committee and getting approval of the appropriate officers. There hadn't been time, I reminded people, if we were to catch this busy man while he was in our area. And in any case offering one's pulpit to a guest speaker was the minister's prerogative in most churches.

Still the disgruntled comments kept reaching me. Instead of dying down as time went by, criticism grew—until at last the real issue surfaced. Bob Walker, it seemed, was an "evangelical," while East Side was a liberal church which did not go in for "emotionalism." That Bob's sermon had not been in the least emotional was obviously not the point. Some deep-seated fear or point of resistance had been touched. I tried to communicate my profound conviction that every church needs both the strength of tradition and the thrust of evangelism. But I had the feeling that a deep and widening chasm had opened at my feet.

There were other disagreements, making waves for a day or a week, nothing that mutual patience and love could not weather. The first serious division occurred over the Wednesday meeting itself. For all the joy and power of these evenings, I had long been aware that only a small fraction of the congregation was taking part—and I'd worried about this. Both from the pulpit and in my pastoral rounds I'd attempted to increase participation.

In spite of a notable lack of success in these recruitment efforts, I was totally unprepared for the amount of resentment that I now learned the meetings had aroused. Words like "exclusive" and "private" began to trickle back to Alice or me—even, from one irate lady: "secret sessions." I searched memory and conscience to see if there was anything to these accusations. The place and hour was posted in the church entrance and announced each Sunday in the church bulletin. Nevertheless it was clear that a large number of people felt left out, excluded from some select "in" group.

Had we who attended the meetings fallen into the trap of considering ourselves "better," or more spiritual, or more committed than those who didn't? Of all the ways we wound and dishonor the Body of Christ I'd always dreaded most such spiritual cliques.

I was thinking of this as I walked home one afternoon when Alice met me at the door of our house with a letter in her hand. With a stricken look on her face she handed it to me. It was from a young couple who had been members of our Toronto prayer meeting.

"I guess you've heard the tragic news about Irene Corbett," the letter began. "Earl seems to be taking her death very well, but I think he would like to hear from you."

Slowly I sank into the chair nearest the door.

"Irene had been doing so well," the letter continued, "that we all had hopes for her complete healing." But apparently the seizures had commenced again, more vicious than ever, and no amount of medication had any effect on them. Earl was afraid to leave her alone while he was at work so Irene was at her sister's home when it happened.

"We think a seizure must have struck as she stood at the top of the basement stairs. She fell before anyone could catch her and her head struck the basement floor. She died in the hospital without regaining consciousness . . . ."

I let the letter drop from my fingers without reading the rest. I felt Alice's hand on my shoulder. "I'm sorry, honey," she said.

I sighed and stood up. "Poor Earl, I guess he's been too upset to write." I paced the living room feeling numb inside, trying to adjust to the news.

Why? I wondered, when her healing had been so close. Why? What had robbed her of it, robbed her of life itself? I suddenly felt responsible in some way for her death. After all, I had been her pastor for three years. Under my ministry she had learned of the healing power of Jesus Christ. She had taken part in the power-packed prayer meetings where miracles had happened, only to be denied a miracle of her own. Perhaps if I had given her more personal attention, or had prayed more fervently . . .

Alice seemed to know what I was thinking. "Don't blame yourself, Don," she said gently. "You did everything you knew to do. We all did."

That evening I sat down and wrote a long letter to Earl, trying to say all the appropriate, helpful things; truths I believed but certainly didn't feel at the time.

When my depression had still not lifted the following morning, I began to worry. I had lost church members before; such events are a part of every pastor's life. Besides, Irene, while a close friend, had not actually been a pastoral responsibility of mine for almost two years. Nevertheless, her death seemed somehow indicative of all the failures in my ministry. I began to appraise my work in Sharon in terms of negatives, reminding myself that in a congregation of over six hundred members, only a few dozen were finding meaningful spiritual answers to their needs, that my ministry was either not reaching the majority of my parishioners or—worse—making them feel outcasts and second-class church members. I knew this was an unhealthy train of thought but I couldn't break out of it.

It was as if, during the night, something I seemed powerless to control had settled upon me. As the days went by and it failed to lift, I found my ministry changing from one of joy and effectiveness to one of dogged endurance.

This was bad enough, but in addition, my low frame of mind opened the door for the recurrence of a more acute problem, the one I had felt stirring the night I had driven Irene Corbett home. That sense of dread, of haunting inner terror with no real name.

For as long as I could remember, there had been periods when this specter had risen within me. What made it particularly frightening was that I never knew when it would appear, only that it would come. Nameless, powerful, relentless, in its grip even the most routine tasks seemed to require Herculean effort. I would pray against it, I would bring my intellect to bear against it, I would seek counseling. Nothing helped. Finally, I would be reduced to a state of miserable hanging-on until the thing ran its course. It could last a few minutes, a few hours, a few days. Sometimes free of it for months—as I had recently been—I would dare to hope it was gone forever. But it always came back.

This time it reappeared one afternoon as I was on my way to make my regular pastoral calls at the hospital. Driving through the streets of Sharon, I suddenly felt a sense of terror at the thought of entering the hospital building. Ridiculous! I was in and out of there half a dozen times a week! Nevertheless, as I approached the parking lot the fear grew so strong I had to drive around the block twice before forcing myself to turn in.

I got out of the car, slammed the door so hard a woman nearby turned to stare at me, and walked toward the hospital entrance. "I can do all things through Christ which strengtheneth me," I said aloud.

"Did you speak to me?" a man standing on the hospital steps inquired.

"Just talking to myself," I said with a nervous smile, and pushed my way through the door. As the sweetish antiseptic hospital odors struck me I stopped short. My stomach churned: for a moment I thought I would be sick right there in the foyer. I plunged back through the doors and took a deep breath of fresh cold air, trying to ignore the curious stare of the man on the steps.

"Get hold of yourself, Basham," I thought. "You've been in this hospital hundreds of times." I knew the fear really had nothing to do with the building or the people in it; rather, it was something originating in me. Still I could not go in. I stood there on the steps for two or three minutes feeling painfully self-conscious.

Then taking another deep breath I turned and re-entered the building. Acknowledging with a nod of my head the receptionist's polite, "Good afternoon, Reverend," I strode to the elevator. Two hours and eight visits later I left the hospital and headed for home nursing a giant headache.

"Alice, where's the aspirin?" were my first words. I walked into the kitchen carefully since any sudden movement increased the pounding in my head.

"Another rough day?" Alice said, counting four white tablets into my hand.

I nodded. "That old fear bugaboo hit again. At the hospital." I looked at Alice over the rim of my glass. "Can you imagine what it was like, trying to minister to sick people while I was having such a battle myself?"

Downing the aspirin, I headed for the living room, turned on the television, and slumped into the nearest chair.

The next morning wasn't much better. The fear was gone—it had crawled back into whatever hiding place it inhabited between attacks—but the knowledge that this was an area where my Christianity seemed powerless simply added to my state of depression. From the time I got out of bed that morning, nothing went right. The children were slower than usual getting dressed. Which made breakfast even more hectic than usual. Which meant that by the time I left for my office I was in such a funk that I forgot to kiss Alice goodbye.

It was all the children's fault of course, not my own. The funk had nothing to do with the unpleasant trip to the bank I would have to make in a few hours. "What a lousy way to start a day," I mumbled as I unlocked the door of my study and let myself in. What a dank and gray-smelling place this church was, anyway! I sat down at my desk and flipped open my Bible, well-worn from previous days when I had found satisfaction in its pages. Perhaps it would be helpful to read a psalm. But after five minutes I snapped the Bible shut; David, that morning, seemed far too spiritual for me. So I turned to work on my sermon, but my notes were as dry and lifeless as they had been the day before.

I leaned back in my chair and stared out the window. Did all ministers have to go through these periods of depression? What had happened to the joy and victory I'd known those final months in Toronto, and for the first year at Sharon?

Did every pastor struggle through the rounds, carrying out his high calling as a dull routine? Of course he did—at least for short times. But . . . I kept thinking how I'd been an ordained minister for almost fifteen years, yet only on rare occasions had even approached the level of effectiveness I dreamed of in seminary. So few people through the years seemed to have been helped, none lately. How could I go on preaching victory when my own life currently showed nothing but frustration?

My eyes fell upon a stack of books on my desk, all treating various aspects of the charismatic renewal. I shoved them around so that I wouldn't see the titles. They only made me feel worse. Up until a few weeks ago, I had found them exciting and helpful. In fact, I had begun work on a book manuscript of my own. Now I felt like a hypocrite even having them on my desk.

Slouched in my chair that morning I could not see that these very frustrations were shortly going to crowd me into a spiritual discovery. It would be a discovery which would set me free from many of my own bondages, and at the same time catapult me into a ministry far more demanding than any I had dreamed of.

At the time I could see none of God's hand in what was happening. I sighed and stood up.

"No sense feeling sorry for yourself, Basham," I muttered as I paced up and down my study. But making the statement did not change the fact. I was in a mood for self-pity, so I kept it rolling, looking for things to complain about. I stopped in front of a picture on the wall. The Hillcrest Church, Toronto. Not only did it recall Irene's tragic death, but other unpleasant memories as well. I recalled how one member of that prosperous congregation, knowing full well the modest salary the church was paying me, still acted surprised that I did not hire a housekeeper. "It would make things so much easier for Alice."

"Don't you know," I said to that memory, "that five dollars in the hands of a preacher buys no more hamburger than it does in the hands of a bank president?"

During the months of spiritual victory, I had scarcely thought about finances; now all my old money worries returned in force. Even at seminary Alice and I had been aware of how little ministers make, and our years in the pastorate had not changed the think-lack pattern. Salary increases had been more than offset by our fast-growing family; only by constant scrimping had we managed to stay out of debt.

Well, almost out of debt. We had long since resorted to the awkward but necessary ruse of consolidating our obligations. When our bills reached a critical level, I would borrow $500 from the bank and settle our accounts. Then as we retired the loan the bills would accumulate once more until by the time the loan was repaid—we had to borrow all over again. Thus we kept our creditors happy, the bank happy, and ourselves barely afloat.

And this morning I was going to the bank once more. Grabbing my hat and coat I left the office, climbed into the car, and headed downtown. It was the second such trip in six months. Our financial situation had become acute since we moved to Sharon. We were living as frugally as before, but our oldest daughter, Cindi, had entered high school and Lisa had started kindergarten; I couldn't tell which was harder on the wardrobe.

Steering through the morning traffic I fed my resentment with reflections that the whole system was unfair. A clergyman had to have as much education as other professionals; he carried as much responsibility; but he received only a fraction of the income. Sanitation workers were earning as much as I did.

Nor did the thought of the meeting where I was due that noon do anything to raise my spirits as I sat on a bench outside the personal loan department. It would be part of the irrelevant make-work which plagued everyone in the church, clergy and lay people alike. Activity which did not meet the real needs of people. Activity for the sake of activity. And most of the time, I admitted ruefully to myself, East Side Church was no better than any other. Prayer meetings and Bible study notwithstanding, we spent much more time working at "food, fun, and fellowship" (how I'd come to despise that trinity!) than we did working at our relationship to God and one another. Right now we were in the process of holding endless committee meetings to find ways to raise money to build the new wing where we could have more rooms to hold more meetings.

Why did we hide behind a smokescreen of busywork like this? In my gloom it almost seemed to me that there was some great silent conspiracy at work to prevent our church—any church—from ministering at deep significant levels by keeping us tormented by trivia.

But the meeting this noon was not, for once, on behalf of the East Side Building Drive. It was the monthly clergymen's luncheon —and it was at these affairs that I often felt most keenly the unreality of what I was doing. While I was still in seminary I had become aware of the fact that I was being groomed for a role. I was not to be myself, I was to be a Minister, if you please, a Reverend. At the end of seven years of training I was no longer just a Christian named Don Basham, I was the Reverend Don Wilson Basham, B.A., B.D.—a man properly equipped to play the ministerial game.

But it was a game in which we were the first losers. I knew that my current depression stemmed, at base, from a faulty relationship with God. But it was almost impossible for me to talk about this, especially to other ministers. The rules of the game called for soft-pedaling "spiritual" answers to personal problems. Be efficient, be friendly, and hardly ever talk about God. That was the formula.

At last the loan officer summoned me to his desk. Many forms and questions later I left the bank with $500 credited to my account, and my eye on the clock. I was due right now at the luncheon where the ministerial game would be in full swing. Game time was twelve noon, the playing field the dining room of a nearby restaurant, the players twelve local clergymen. The name of the game was, "Ministerial Fellowship." Originally I had hoped at these meetings to get to know my colleagues more personally, but it hadn't turned out that way. Even in these informal gatherings we carefully wore our masks. I looked around the table as I walked in and sat down, thinking of the problems we all knew we had, problems we never shared, problems we never prayed about together.

The minister opposite me, new in our community, had divorced his wife during his former pastorate. His present church had hired him only under pressure from their conference hierarchy. After several months he was still struggling to find a way to minister to a hostile congregation.

Next to him a quiet, gray-haired minister whose wife lay ill in the hospital with terminal cancer listened to his account of a Sunday school awards program without comment.

Beyond both of them sat a stocky balding pastor with a clerical collar, a booming voice, and two delinquent teen-age daughters.

Beside me the cheerful extrovert who pastored a small church and taught high school English in a nearby town kept his jovial smile in place. The smile, which never quite covered the pain in his eyes, had been there since the day his wife had been admitted to a mental institution.

Everyone in the room, I noted, nursed some private misery. I knew that these men were struggling as sincerely as I was with their problems, but that each of us seemed shackled by defeat. And all the while our professionalism conspired to keep us from sharing our deepest concerns.

Well, today I was desperate enough that I resolved to step out from behind the mask. It was going to take some maneuvering, for the game was going as scheduled: the jovial joke-telling, the careful adherence to small talk. Nevertheless, I was determined to make the effort. Over dessert I began.

"You know, fellows, I need your help." I intended to talk about the fear: somehow I found myself saying, "I've been in a real slump lately. My ministry seems like a waste of time. I feel as if, well, as if I've been deserted by God. Any of you ever feel like that?"

The room grew suddenly very quiet. I waited for the first words of understanding. The man across from me glanced at the minister sitting next to him, then down at his coffee cup. I tried again.

"Lately I have the feeling that I am just performing . . . going through the motions without coming to grips with anything real. It's as if I'm playing some big meaningless game . . . know what I mean?"

I glanced around the room again, red-faced. I had not thought this would be so hard. Not one eye met mine. The dishes on the table seemed to have some huge fascination. Miserably, I tried once more. This time I told about the recurring fear and the experience at the hospital.

"I just don't seem to be able to do anything about this fear. I wish you men would comment. I know it's not on your agenda today, but I really need—"

The extrovert next to me suddenly reached over and slapped me on the back. "Basham, you're taking yourself too seriously! What you need is a day off! Get out of town for a few hours! You'll snap out of it!"

He turned to the others. "Say, come to think of it, that's a great idea! Why don't we plan an all-day retreat? Just the twelve of us?" Then, as if frightened by his own impulsiveness, he added, "Of course, I'm too busy to do it any time soon." He pulled out his little black date book. "How about right after Easter?"

I watched as all the men pulled out their little black books, all agreeing that their schedules were too crowded now, but maybe after Easter it would work out.

The trouble was, their schedules *were* crowded. I knew their dilemma for it was mine too. The constant demands on our time, the pressure to fulfill an endless number of organizational duties as if they were profoundly important. The need to appear happy, wise, and successful, even if we weren't. The feeling of guilt when we took time off for ourselves and families. The fear that if we let our own weaknesses show, we would somehow be betraying our calling.

I listened as the men resumed their earnest small talk, carefully steering around my plea for help. I knew many of them understood what I meant and sympathized with my struggle, but the rules of the game just didn't allow us to acknowledge these things. Like me, they were caught in the system.

Finally, I could stand it no longer. With a murmured apology about pressing pastoral duties I hurried from the room. It was a moment before I realized that someone had followed me. A gaunt, balding man in his fifties, I knew Chester Bates as the pastor of a small evangelical church in Sharon, noted for its biblical fundamentalism and acrobatic, top-of-the-lungs preaching. But his voice was gentle as he spoke to me on the sidewalk outside the restaurant.

"Don, I didn't want you to get away without sharing something which might help you." I listened, grateful for even one man who would discard the mask.

"I realize that you and most of the others in there," he shrugged in the direction of the room we had just left, "have far more education than I have. But the problem you described sounded so similar to a period I went through some years back . . . ." He paused and peered earnestly at me through wire-rimmed spectacles. "Do you know what proved to be more help to me than anything else?"

I shook my head.

"It was the realization that I had a personal enemy who was out to undermine my ministry."

I stared at him blankly. "But Chester, I don't know anyone here in Sharon who would—"

Chester Bates shook his head. "That's not what I mean. I mean a spiritual adversary. An 'enemy in high places.' The Bible calls him Satan. Once I understood who was opposing my ministry . . . ."

It was an effort to keep my face straight. Surely the man didn't literally . . . . But as he continued talking it was apparent that he did. Here we were, two presumably sane adults, standing across the street from an Esso station on a Tuesday afternoon and discussing Satan as though he might come strolling by at any minute.

"Chester," I interrupted at last, "I appreciate your sympathy and concern, I really do." I hoped I didn't sound as condescending as I felt. "It means a great deal to me." I pumped his hand too energetically and sprinted for my car.

"That's the trouble with biblical literalists," I fumed as I roared away. A pat answer for everything, so we're saved the discomfort of thinking. The man belonged in the Middle Ages! Satan indeed! What a very convenient excuse—when our own lack of faith or laziness or bad planning spoils something: "the devil" is at fault!

My fundamentalist friend had meant well, but all he had done was to add irritation to my depression. Back home I swallowed some more aspirin and plunked myself down in front of the TV. More and more often in recent weeks I had found myself attempting to escape my problems by watching reruns of old movies. It didn't help but I watched them anyway. The more frustrated I felt, the more television I watched.

By suppertime I had convinced myself that I didn't really have to be at the boring interchurch planning committee that evening. When I switched off the set at 1:00 A.M., I got to thinking again of that afternoon's ministerial meeting. Each of these men, I knew, must have understood my cry, because each had some crushing problem of his own. Yet only one had offered any kind of advice, and it was too far out to consider seriously.

"Nevertheless," I sighed as I undressed in the darkened bedroom, "something seems to have a stranglehold on the church. And on me as well."

3

The One-Eyed Monster

LOOKING back I can see that each of these elements was part of a mammoth puzzle: (1) my baptism in the Holy Spirit; (2) my taste of a power-filled and joy-filled ministry and the frustration of not being able to maintain what I had tasted; (3) growing awareness that my colleagues in the professional ministry were powerless too, and thus forced to play games; and (4) dismay at my own recurring personal hang-ups. All—I see now—were part of a preparation time through which the Lord had to put me before I would be ready to go ahead in a ministry which would at times be excruciatingly difficult, pioneering, and lonesome. There were two chief lessons that I had to learn before He could send me to that demanding frontier. I had yet to learn what it was to be disciplined; I had yet to learn what it was really to trust God.

The lesson in discipline started first. The day after I stayed up until 1:00 A.M. watching television, I could scarcely drag myself out of bed. Alice noticed my silence during breakfast and, as I left for the church, gave me an extra kiss.

"Don't forget Whom we belong to."

I kissed her back. How many times in our marriage had we comforted each other with the reminder that no matter how rough things became, we still belonged to Jesus Christ!

Once in the office, however, my depression returned. I had to force myself through the usual administrative responsibilities; clearing the usual items on the calendar with the church secretary, taking the usual phone calls, making a few notes toward Sunday's sermon.

In the afternoon was a round of pastoral calls and another visit to the hospital. Thank God there was no return of the fear— just a plodding gray weariness about everything I did. Tonight was prayer meeting at church, the time I usually looked forward to all week; this evening even that prospect seemed dull and pointless.

Before leaving for the church I switched on the seven o'clock news: a man needs to keep up with what's happening in the world. Actually I knew my real motive: I wanted to see what was coming up on the TV movie. Following the news there was always a preview of the night's show. Sure enough, tonight it was an exciting film about airplanes. Now I happen to be an aviation buff. As a boy, I made model airplanes, as a teen-ager read books and magazines about flying, and as a young adult took flying lessons and earned my pilot's license. Watching the preview of daredevil escapades in the sky, I became suddenly and unreasonably furious at the prayer meeting and everyone who would be there: "Why does it have to be tonight?" Then I began a bit of mental scheming. The TV program didn't begin until 9:00 P.M. If I cut the opening prayers short, and if only Elsie Krieder didn't get started on her dreams . . . .

I said a hurried goodbye to Alice and climbed into the car. The tires screamed a bit as I accelerated and took the first corner too sharp, racing the stop light. About half way to the church, I slowed down. A movie was doing this to me. A silly movie.

Television had such a hold on me that I was prepared to put on an act in front of the people I prayed with, planning to cut short a meeting which might be tremendously important to somebody there.

I pulled over to the curb. Disgusted at my own rebelliousness, I shut off the engine. "Lord, I vow to you at this moment that I will not shorten the meeting just for a stupid movie."

And I didn't. After everyone else went home at 10:00 P.M., I walked into the empty auditorium and played the piano all by myself, singing hymns in a loud voice until 11:00 o'clock when the movie would be over.

Even as I put on my coat and turned out the church lights I knew that this was a turning point for me. I walked toward the car. A cold mist had been falling all evening and it was beginning to freeze. Cautiously I drove the slippery streets home, put the car in the garage, and let myself into the house. Alice and the children were asleep. Hanging my coat in the closet I headed for the stairs, loosening my tie as I went. With one foot on the bottom step I stopped. "No. I won't go to bed tonight until I get this thing settled."

I walked to the window. The pale light from the lamppost at the corner cast spectral, long-legged shadows from the foot of each ice-covered tree and shrub. A freezing rain, whipped by the wind, rattled and scratched at the glass. The weather outside matched my inner climate to perfection. I sat near the window and recounted the problems I was struggling with: financial worries, my disgust with professionalism in the ministry, my fight against fear, and my frustrating and useless attempts to escape the whole mess by watching television. At that moment all of my problems seemed exemplified by my morbid fascination with the TV set.

I glanced across the room. There it sat like a fat smug Buddha, staring at me with its huge darkened eye. "But Lord," I said aloud, "the problem is not television. The problem is me. Lord, I'm no good this way. Please help me!"

And there under the gaze of the television set, a quiet majestic Presence enveloped me. I felt a peace I had not known for weeks. I knew in that instant that the Lord was with me in my struggle. Whatever I was struggling against, it was not God. He was on my side, neither condemning nor criticizing me—only yearning for me to come to Him. I felt overwhelmed with the sense of His love.

Out of the peace that invaded me was born a small shining resolve. By God's grace I would climb out of the despondency I was in. I took a deep breath and that inner resolve broke forth in words.

"To hell with television!"

Startled by the loudness of my own voice, I glanced at the ceiling, wondering if I had disturbed Alice and the children upstairs. Above me everything remained still. With that renunciation I knew that the problem of television no longer existed. I couldn't explain it. Just as I had known earlier that television was a trap for me, so I now knew that I was free.

But then a peculiar thing happened. It is something I have never forgotten over the years, as I have met other temptations, other traps. The Presence remained with me in that room. It seemed to be waiting for something.

I felt as if I were being edged toward a second step. It was as if the renouncing of a negative habit was not enough. I felt that I also had to make some positive commitment before my victory was assured. How often in the ministry which was about to unfold would I recall the lesson which I learned that winter night with a fog freezing on the trees outside. *Getting rid of the negatives in our life is but half the struggle: each subtraction must be followed immediately by an addition.*

I heard myself saying, "I'll start getting up at five o'clock in the morning. I'll spend two hours with you, Lord." Again I was surprised at my own words. Yet having spoken them, I felt committed.

I stood up and looked out the window. The wind had died down and the freezing rain had stopped falling. "It will be clear in the morning," I thought. As I headed for the stairs, I glanced once more at the television set in the corner. It seemed smaller, somehow.

4

Five O'Clock in the Morning

I DON'T mean to indicate that the "addition" part of this spiritual mathematics was easy. It wasn't. When the alarm clock went off at 5:00 the next morning I couldn't imagine what I had set it for. Then as my hand fumbled for the off button, I remembered. "This is stupid," I groaned. "It's not going to do any good."

"What is it, honey?" Alice's voice was soft and warm with sleep.

"Something I've got to do," I said vaguely. "Go back to sleep."

Still thinking how nice it would be to roll over for another two hours, I struggled out of the covers, got into my clothes and groped my way downstairs. The living room was pitch dark and singularly uninviting as I viewed it from the bottom of the stairs at 5:05 that morning. I switched on a lamp at the end of the couch and sat down with my Bible. Waves of sleepiness washed over me.

"This is no good," I thought, after my head bobbed forward for the fifth time. I switched positions and got down on my knees, leaning forward on the couch. Five minutes later I got up and walked around. I went to the refrigerator and poured a glass of fruit juice. I read the Bible aloud, hoping that the sound of my own voice would keep me awake. At last, after a year had passed, I heard Alice and the children stirring. All in all it was a pretty miserable first attempt.

The next morning was just as bad. And the next. Even after a week there had been no change. The struggle to get up was just as intense, the battle to stay awake just as fierce. I was tempted to go back on my commitment, but some stubborn resolve held me to it: each morning I managed, somehow, to overrule the protests of mind and body and climb out of bed.

Then, late in the second week, things began to break.

Although getting up was hard as ever, on about the twelfth morning the living room seemed to welcome me. I felt a quiet assurance that heaven watched and approved of my efforts to break out of the slump. Little by little, my spirit responded to the new routine, and the stillness of those early hours began to beckon attractively. The initial shock of rising never diminished, but once up and dressed, I found myself almost eager to begin prayer. Being in the presence of God nourished my thirsty soul like sunlight nourishing a garden.

As a result, things began to change outwardly as well. Gradually, vigor and strength were restored to my preaching. I became more patient with the tedium of dry, ineffectual meetings. The headaches which had plagued me for several weeks disappeared. I turned once more to the manuscript of the book I was writing: the personal narrative of my search for the power of God's Holy Spirit.

One morning I was pacing up and down my office at the church struggling with this manuscript when suddenly I stopped short. For the first time I saw the possibility that the events which had been occurring in my life were all going somewhere.

In front of me sat the pile of books about the charismatic

movement. They had remained on my desk just as I had left them weeks ago, titles turned away so that I would not be reminded of Christians whose lives seemed to be filled with victory and power. Now in a slightly self-conscious gesture I turned the titles around again. For I was suddenly glimpsing all that was happening as part of a pattern.

Perhaps after the baptism in the Holy Spirit we always face a time of perplexity until we take the steps we are intended to take. The baptism is the time when God endows His people with power. Doubtless, in God's ecology, each of us is supposed to use that power in some special ministry in the Body of Christ: healing, evangelism, prophecy . . . .

But if for some reason we have not learned what our ministry is supposed to be, or if we cannot use our new power because of a local situation in the church, wouldn't we be left with a terrible sense of frustration? Was the valley I had been going through, then, God's way of showing me I had not yet found His direction for my work?

One Sunday morning right in the middle of the service I felt prompted to change sermon topics. I very rarely did this. Yet on this particular morning, obedient to my prompting, I pushed my sermon notes aside and spoke informally about our need to trust the word of God. As I spoke, my attention kept being drawn to a member of the congregation, Mrs. Abel Stern. Mrs. Stern was a very large lady who always sat in the third row. During the sermon this morning she began shaking her head either affirmatively or negatively depending on whether or not she agreed with what I was saying.

"To know God's will, read His word," I told the congregation. "For the will of God and the word of God agree. Everything He promises in His word, we as Christians have the right to claim. God still speaks to us today through the Bible." I found myself illustrating this impromptu sermon with personal references to occasions when Scripture had spoken directly to me in a most powerful way. Mrs. Stern's headshaking became more and more negative.

After the service I took my post at the door—part of the preacher's game, giving him an opportunity to be pleasant to the maximum number of people with the minimum amount of involvement. With a dread I could not account for I saw Mrs. Stern work her way toward me. Her lips were set in a thin angry line. I had no way of knowing that in fact she was going to be one of God's direction markers.

Ignoring my outstretched hand, Mrs. Stern began in a loud voice: "Of course one expects ministers to talk about the Bible, Reverend Williams—er, Basham." Though I had been at East Side for over two years, Mrs. Stern persisted in calling me by the name of my predecessor. "But God also speaks to us in other ways. Personally, I find Bible reading tedious. I much prefer to have God speak to me directly during my prayer time."

Wincing at the condescension in her tone, I murmured something about checking out our individual revelations against the written word.

"I know the voice of God when He speaks to me," Mrs. Stern announced. And ignoring my still outstretched hand, she swept past me and out the door.

I greeted the rest of the line with only half my attention. Mrs. Stern's hostility confused me. She was not like this to everyone, only me. She was in fact known throughout the church for her many acts of kindness and service. Why was I the target for her anger? Was it because I had not been sufficiently impressed with her spirituality? At every church gathering she had some new "comprehension" to share; to me it often sounded offbeat and eccentric. Once, with a strange dreamy expression on her face, she had confided that her relationship to God had become so intimate that it was like a physical love affair, so that any attempt of her husband to touch her physically produced feelings of revulsion. I had suggested to Mrs. Stern that such sensuous experiences did not necessarily stem from God, meaning—at the time—only that they might be coming from her own subconscious. But though I had made this comment in private, to spare her embarrassment, and had put it as tactfully as I knew how, it was apparent that she had never forgiven me.

The following Wednesday I heard a story which encouraged and at the same time puzzled me. In my pastoral calling I stopped in the late afternoon at the home of a young couple who, I knew, were having financial difficulties. The wife greeted me at the door with unexpected warmth.

"Do come in," she said, showing me to the only soft chair in the sparsely furnished living room. "I wish John were here. He works the late shift at the mill you know. But I have something important to tell you. Your sermon Sunday saved our marriage."

"Really? How?"

"Well, you see, my husband gambles, or at least he did. We've lost thousands of dollars in the last few years because of it. Whenever I'd complain about it, he would just laugh and say, 'I can't help it honey, it's my gambling demon.'

"I finally got so fed up," she went on, "that I decided to divorce him. I was planning to leave Monday but wanted to attend East Side one more time. Sunday night I couldn't sleep for thinking how you said we should live by the word of God. 'Lord,' I said, 'if You wanted to, You could speak to me through Your word right now.' Then I got out my Bible, took a deep breath, and opened it."

The woman's voice grew shaky and tears appeared in her eyes. "The very first words I read were these: 'What God hath joined together let no man put asunder.'"

She shook her head. "I was flabbergasted. I knew it was more than coincidence. The next morning I told John how I'd been planning to leave home because of his gambling until I read that verse. For the first time in our ten years of marriage John cried. Then he said, 'Honey, whatever it is that's been making me gamble, I want to be free of it.' Then he asked Jesus to help him.

"Always in the past, Mr. Basham, John has cashed his paycheck himself; the children and I never saw much of it. But last night"—she blinked back tears of gratitude—"last night he brought his check and gave it to me."

On the way home I found the palms of my hands sweating. The story of the family's reconciliation should have made me feel good—and it did. I was especially grateful that I had followed that impulse to change the sermon topic. But there was something else about the story, something which haunted me. I kept running it over and over in my mind. It was as if God were trying to call my attention to something which I was just not grasping.

About three months after I began my morning prayer discipline, events started to occur which at the time I did not see as nudges from God but, rather, as minor disasters. The first incident took place at a regular meeting of our board of elders, a meeting which began routinely enough. Midway through it, however, Ward Weatherby, an elder who had never voiced any objection to my ministry before, made a critical remark.

"Don," he said with some testiness in his voice, "it seems to me that you have become so preoccupied with what you call the spiritual life of the church that you are neglecting your administrative duties. There's more to running a church than preaching and visiting the sick and conducting a few prayer meetings."

I intended to answer with tact and patience. I had always prided myself on my skill in these situations.

Instead I began to defend my ministry and with every word I seemed to put my foot in my mouth. What began as a quiet discussion developed into a loud argument. The other elders joined in, hurling angry remarks both at Ward Weatherby and at me. To my consternation, the whole meeting fell apart; hostility and antagonism flared everywhere. At last the chairman adjourned what had really ceased to be a meeting. I trudged out to my car and drove home, angry. Not with Ward Weatherby and the others, but with myself.

"And Ward Weatherby's criticisms weren't really all that bad," I confessed to Alice and the children next morning at breakfast. "I don't know how things got out of hand so quickly. It was as if something vicious just swept into the room and blew the meeting sky-high!"

But it was not just the meeting. "Were you able to help the Morleys?" the church secretary asked me as I entered the office a few minutes later.

"The Morleys?" I echoed. They were one of the most active and influential families in the church.

Consternation showed on the secretary's face. "Didn't you see my note on your desk?"

I went into my office. There right in the middle of the desk lay the note. *Harold Morley called—wants to see you—says it's urgent.* "I'll never know how I overlooked that!" I said. (Today, I'm not sure I'd make that statement.)

I immediately drove to the Morley home and apologized. But it was too late. They had needed help yesterday, not now. A rebellious son was threatening to leave home and the Morleys wanted me to talk to him. The boy agreed to wait, but when I didn't show up, he packed his things in disgust and left. The parents were bitter and my excuse that "I didn't get your message" sounded lame, even to me.

"Clobbered again!" I muttered as I drove away from their house.

The next afternoon I had a telephone call from Mrs. Stern.

She wanted to see me immediately. She opened the door even before I could ring the bell.

"I wasn't sure you would come after what happened with the Morleys," she said. Bad news moves fast! "But that's not what I wanted to talk to you about, Reverend Williams. I know what I'm about to say may sound strange," she paused. "I . . . I would like you to pray for me." It obviously cost her a great deal to make the request.

"Pray? About what?" I asked gently.

"Well, it may sound silly, but I've had a most awful feeling lately . . . . A feeling that *something* is determined to keep me from obeying God. Something . . . evil!" And she gave a little shudder.

"We all have times like that, Mrs. Stern," I answered in my best pastoral tone. "Man is basically selfish and the Christian life is a continual struggle to—"

But obviously, Mrs. Stern was in no mood for a lecture. She dismissed my words with a curt wave of the hand. "I know all that. What I'm describing is altogether different. It's more like . . . like . . ." Even as I watched her struggle for the right word, a shadow seemed to pass across her face. An angry light flickered in her eyes; her hands clenched. Suddenly and unreasonably I found myself remembering Irene Corbett that night in the Toronto prayer meeting. Jerking my head to shake off the impression, I took out my New Testament.

"Let me read a passage of Scripture which may help, Mrs. Stern," I said as I turned to the book of Romans. "Even Paul, you know, had to struggle against self.

So I find it to be a law that when I want to do right, evil lies close at hand. For I delight in the law of God, in my inmost self, but I see in my members another law at war with the law of my mind and making me captive to the law of sin which dwells in my members. (Romans 7:21–22 RSV)

"But Paul called on the Lord for help and received it," I concluded. "And so can we. We can ask God to help you in this."

Mrs. Stern seemed unconvinced, but she agreed to let me pray. "I think," I said as I concluded the prayer, "that you'll find things better tomorrow."

But the next day Mrs. Stern was not better. She telephoned me four times in as many days to report that she still felt harassed, that my prayers were doing no good. After the fourth call I was thoroughly discouraged. The next step, I knew, would be to refer Mrs. Stern to good psychological counseling. Perhaps the time had come for that. I decided I would spend the following morning's prayer vigil seeking guidance for Mrs. Stern. Little did I realize that when that hour came I would be caught up in a desperate intercession for my own life.

Right now, I had a sermon to prepare. The notes lay on my desk, untouched since the night of the disastrous elders' meeting. The text seemed to mock me, considering the events of the last few days: "I am come that they might have life, and that they might have it more abundantly." Was the Morleys' son experiencing abundant life? Was Mrs. Stern? Why was this Bible promise not being realized at East Side Church in 1966?

Even as I asked the question, it came to me that I was quoting only a portion of that verse. I flipped open my Bible to the tenth chapter of John and found it.

The thief cometh not, but for to steal, and to kill, and to destroy: I am come that they might have life, and that they might have it more abundantly.

A thief . . . the thief cometh. Funny, that was exactly what it felt like. As though something were robbing us of the joy and

peace and power Jesus clearly told us could be ours. I gave a
dry little grimace at my own thought. "In a minute you'll be
sounding like Chester Bates," I reproached myself.

But then—what was this "thief" Jesus spoke of, this force or
entity so opposite to Himself? Oh, of course I knew what His
hearers back in those days understood. At seminary we had
studied the first-century world, with its naïve cosmology and its
concept of a personal devil. The "thief," to the unlettered Pales-
tinian peasant, would have meant quite simply "Satan" or "Beelzebub." Our more sophisticated age, of course, recognized it as another of Jesus' vivid metaphors, concrete and picturesque, ideally
suited to the mentality of His day.

In seminary I learned that the notion of Satan as a literal
being, as an actual personification of evil, was an outgrowth of
ancient theology, stemming from the biblical writers' anthropo-
morphic view of good and evil. Modern theology does not em-
brace any such primitive dualism, a reality divided between a
Good God and a bad god. There is only one All-Encompassing
Source; the Ultimate Ground of All Being.

Yet even as I repeated the unassailable phrases, certain nagging doubts which I had long kept submerged came floating to
the surface. For to be honest I had to admit that the same theology which dismissed personalized evil and the myth of Satan
also left no room for the miraculous gifts and ministries of the
Holy Spirit, which had so profoundly touched my own life.

Yet how could any trained mind seriously entertain the thought
of Satan as an actual being? The spooky idea of a negative personality out there some place—someone bent on killing and
stealing and destroying—this simply did not fit in with any modern understanding of the subconscious and societal sources of our
difficulties. It sounded like the creation of a paranoid mind:
someone's out there to get me! There was a form of mental ill-

ness which saw an Enemy behind every lamppost, interpreted every mishap as a persecution by the Evil One. I had met one or two such people in my life; they were pitiful figures.

I snapped my Bible shut and stood up. I had preached on that "abundant life" text in Toronto. I would simply get out the earlier sermon outline and work from it.

The next morning the alarm went off at its usual spine-jarring 5:00 o'clock. In a few minutes I was settled on the couch, the Bible open on my lap, Mrs. Stern's problem occupying my mind. The first inkling of trouble came like a cold film on my face. At first, I thought I was having another fear attack like the one at the hospital. But—it was not like that. This was something different, something far worse. It was as though a smothering invisible shroud were slowly dropping over me, cutting off the air. I struggled for breath, I tried to stand up, but I was wrapped in the suffocating presence.

"What's happening?" I cried. "Oh, God! Help me!"

My lungs strained for air, my heart hammered in my throat. No escape, the thought kept coming. There's no escape. I made a despairing effort to hurl myself from the sofa, to burst out of this weird, clinging thing, but my legs would not move. It was unbelievable, but I was dying. Dying here in my living room with Alice just upstairs.

"It's a heart attack," I thought. "I'm having a coronary . . . ."

I clung to consciousness. My body and mind grew numb and then beyond the numbness something like a blizzard of ice stung every cell in my body. I shivered uncontrollably and broke into cold perspiration. Summoning the last bit of strength I could muster, I cried aloud, "Lord Jesus, I will not let you go."

In desperation I wrapped my arms around my body and hugged myself, as though I would hold my very life within me.

Then, just as a tornado wreaks its havoc and rages swiftly on, the smothering pall receded. I drew a long, rasping breath. "Thank you, Lord, thank you," I gasped.

As my breath and my heartbeat returned to normal, I thought, "I must get to a doctor!" But even as I was starting for the phone I knew that the attack was really over. A sense of stillness spread through me. By the time the family arose at 7:00 A.M. I was feeling quite fit, with nothing left of the experience except the frightening memory of it. Several times during the day I considered seeing a physician, but each time I decided against it. Neither did I tell Alice. At least, not until the second time.

The second attack came a week later. I awakened as always at 5:00 A.M. Even as I reached to shut off the alarm clock came that rising sense of dread and foreboding.

"It's coming! It's coming!" I thought. My arm was stretched toward the nightstand, the alarm clock still ringing when the suffocating airlessness descended. Once again it seemed impossible either to breathe or to pray through the stifling thing closing around me. I wanted to run—out the door, down the stairs, out of the house—anywhere. With my last strength I hauled myself to a sitting position. Alice switched on the light.

"What is it, honey?" There was fright in her voice.

"Don't know! I feel strange!"

Alice came around the bed and shut off the alarm. She sat beside me, taking my hands in hers. I leaned weakly against her shoulder as the awful sleet storm knifed its way through my body. Once again I heard myself saying, "Jesus, I will never let you go!" I gripped Alice's hands so hard I felt her wince. Then, like the first attack, this one subsided as quickly as it had come.

"Thank God," I sighed, sitting up straight once more.

Alice put her hand on my forehead. "Don! What's the matter!"

"Nothing," I said, still taking grateful gulps of air. "Nothing—now."

"But, Don, something's very much the matter! You get back under the covers while I call the doctor." She reached for the telephone.

"No, don't do that! It isn't necessary. I tell you I'm all right." Alice put down the receiver reluctantly.

"What on earth was it?"

"Just some weird sort of dizzy spell, I guess. But I'm fine now." I stood up and began to get dressed. "I'm going downstairs. You go back to sleep."

Alice argued with me for a while longer, then insisted on accompanying me downstairs to the living room. We spent the next two hours alternately thanking God for bringing me through the fearsome attack and pleading with Him to reveal to us what was going on. Why, when my personal relationship with Him had become more meaningful than ever, was I being subject to these bizarre attacks?

That afternoon Mrs. Stern came to my office at church, very agitated. The tone of her voice, even the appearance of her face changed and shifted rapidly as she spoke. When I hinted that I had the names of several qualified psychiatrists, she grew furious. Her last words lingered in the little room.

"I came to *you* for help! Can't you give it to me?"

I leaned back in my chair after she had gone and stared morbidly out the window. So many things were happening lately which seemed to defy my understanding of spiritual principles. I knew without question that a real note of spiritual victory had been struck when I began that early morning prayer vigil. Both from inward and outward evidences, this was apparent.

Yet rising up in the face of this fact was a series of disasters. Take the elders' meeting. I was still baffled over that nasty eruption. Nor was I the only one. In the days following that meeting several of the men had apologized to me for things they had said; they seemed as puzzled as I about what had happened. And that missed appointment with the Morleys! I still could not understand what had blinded me to that note on my desk. The Morleys had not been back in church since the incident.

I bit my lip at the next memory. These strange physical attacks during the morning prayer time! Could it be more than coincidence that they had both taken place when they did? For a fleeting moment I recalled how Irene Corbett's seizures—at least most of them —seemed to take place during prayer meetings.

And finally, my patent inability to help Mrs. Stern. Whatever was plaguing her, it seemed to laugh at my efforts to help her. How could I reconcile the apparent contradiction between my improved personal relationship to God and the series of—well, almost assaults on my ministry?

They were not assaults, of course. I mean, that would suppose someone out there doing the assaulting. It was simply an accident of timing, a series of unfortunate coincidences that happened to fall as I was making progress elsewhere in my ministry. There could hardly be any connection between—and then I recalled something.

Jesus' own ministry. Right at the start, when He had received His Father's approval, and the Holy Spirit had descended upon Him, and He was all ready to set about God's business—what was His very first experience? An encounter with Satan (whatever we in the twentieth century were to understand by this word). But whoever or whatever "Satan" was, it was obvious that *something* had made its appearance at this point which was opposed to His mission. Something which tried to get in and spoil things, to divert Him and get Him off the track. I suspected it was His human nature, or the collective unconscious of the race, or some such influence—but whatever it was, He had suffered an attack on His ministry just as I was doing.

My heart bounded. Even here He had gone before to show the way! In this too He would be the model on which to base our lives. Though the terminology and the intellectual framework might have changed in two thousand years, the basic truth had not. I would read the New Testament to discover how Jesus had dealt with this opposition or negative force—however differently His age and mine understood it.

At 5:04 the next morning, I switched on the lamp by the living-room sofa, picked up a notebook and pencil and opened my Bible, flipping through the Gospels, jotting down passages that dealt with Satan. To my consternation I came face to face almost immediately with a fact even less palatable to the rational mind: while Jesus had perceived His adversary in the wilderness as "Satan" or "the devil," in His ministry He dealt most often not with this entity but with "evil spirits" and "demons"; not with a single enemy but with a plural enemy.

I chewed the end of my pencil over that bit of information. I had the feeling I was opening a kind of Pandora's box. Demons? Evil spirits? Ugly little things running around? The idea repelled me even more than the concept of Satan.

I suppose the one thing that kept me from dropping the whole matter right then was the persistent memory of Irene Corbett. I just couldn't dismiss the idea that something evil had usurped control over her—even as Alice had hinted on that night Irene had behaved so strangely, something that had robbed her of her healing and led to her tragic death. More than anything else I was seeking an answer to why so many prayers for her had failed.

Had I suspected, even for a moment, the drastic effect my investigation was to have on my own life and ministry, I would have left the subject strictly alone.

But I didn't know, and so I read on, filling page after page of the notebook, increasingly amazed to discover what a very high percentage of Jesus' ministry dealt with these "evil spirits." Casting out demons and healing seemed to go hand in hand: "That evening they brought to him many who were possessed with demons; and he cast out the spirits with a word, and healed all who were sick." [Matthew 8:16 RSV]

More upsetting, He seemed to expect His disciples to carry on this dual function. "And he called to him his twelve disciples and gave them authority over unclean spirits, to cast them out, and to heal every disease and every infirmity." [Matthew 10:1 RSV] The disciples did. "The seventy returned with joy, saying, 'Lord, even the demons are subject to us in your name!' " [Luke 10:17 RSV]

These were, of course, I kept reminding myself, the thought forms of His day. Jesus said "demons" or "unclean spirits" when speaking to His followers because these were concepts they understood. To us He would say "psychosomatic ailment" or "schizophrenia" or "psychosis" or what-have-you. And not for the first time I wondered at the inscrutable wisdom of God, with all of history from which to choose, selecting for His incarnation a period and a people which had such outlandish beliefs.

It was the third morning of my research when I noticed something else. Whatever the pathology to which the first century gave the name "demon possession," the approach that Jesus taught worked, and worked instantly. When His disciples acted, people recovered on the spot from the symptoms or behavior which plagued them. For all our seemingly having arrived at a better diagnosis of these problems, we weren't even close to these simple people's performance in dealing with them. I knew of no psychiatrist, no matter how highly trained, who could alleviate psychosomatic symptoms "with a word," or take "authority" over paranoia. His patients got better—when they did—only after slow and costly treatment.

It was just the same paradox as in other branches of medicine. Peter probably knew less than today's ten-year-old about human anatomy, but at his word the lame leaped, while today with all our knowledge we correct lameness—when we do—only with painstaking surgical techniques. I believed in the instantaneous, miraculous kind of healing described in the Bible, as well as in medical healing, because I had seen both happen. By the same token, what about the "casting out" of evil influences on one's mind and body, which was mentioned in the Bible at least as often as healing. Whether I understood it or not, would people be helped? For, to be strictly true to *my* period in history, there was one question I had failed to ask, the only question which makes sense to a scientific and pragmatic age.

Does it work?

Experiment. Observe. Try it and see. These are the methods of my time and my place.

I got up from the couch and stood at the window, watching the trees take shape in the first gray light of dawn. What if, for a few days or a few weeks, I were to act *as if* demons existed? Never mind trying to rationalize it. Just follow the Bible pattern exactly. Do what Jesus did—and see.

5

Sam Jenkins Remembers

WHILE Alice and I were having lunch a few days later, there was a frantic knocking at the back door.

It was Mrs. Stern. I invited her in. She lowered her considerable frame onto one of our narrow kitchen chairs and stared miserably at the floor until Alice tactfully left the room. After a few minutes she raised her eyes.

"Reverend Basham" (no mistaking my name this time!), "something has happened which I don't understand." She paused, drew a shaky breath, and continued. "I was praying this morning when a voice began to speak inside of me. I thought it was God because it was the same whispering I've heard before."

She struggled for composure, then went on. "But this morning the voice began to make lewd suggestions. When I protested it began to curse! It boasted that I belonged to it and that great harm would come to me if I did not obey. . . . What should I do? I'm frightened!"

As calmly as my hammering heart would allow, I said, "Mrs. Stern, from what you've said I think we have to consider the possibility that an evil spirit is tormenting you. Why don't we pray—"

But at the mention of the words "evil spirit" Mrs. Stern jumped to her feet. "I knew I shouldn't have come! I'm getting out of here!" She rushed for the door.

I followed, protesting.

"Mrs. Stern, you mustn't leave when you're so upset. Come back and sit down." I took her arm and tried to steer her toward a chair.

"Don't touch me!" She pulled free. "Leave me alone!" She fled out the door, and across the yard to her car. I went after her.

"Mrs. Stern, please! Come back inside; you're in no condition to drive!"

Searching for a way to regain control of the situation, I thought of removing the key from the ignition. I said nothing. I did not take my eyes from hers and I made no move toward the car. Nevertheless, a crafty expression crossed Mrs. Stern's face.

"Oh, no you don't!" she said.

Jerking the car door open, she reached in and took the keys from the ignition. Then she slammed the car door and dashed across the street to my neighbor's yard where she began trotting back and forth like an animal in a cage, wailing, "Leave me alone! Stay away from me!"

I couldn't believe what was happening. Alice came outside and watched, helpless as I. Nothing in my seminary training, nothing from my courses in pastoral psychology or in my years of experience had taught me the proper way to chase an overwrought woman parishioner around the neighborhood. Cars slowed down. Neighbors stared out their windows. I kept shaking my head and thinking, "This is a bad dream."

For a while longer I begged Mrs. Stern to come inside, but she only paced faster and wailed louder. Not knowing what else to do, I finally nodded to Alice and we both went back into the house. As soon as I had closed the door, Mrs. Stern scurried back across the street, jumped into her car, and roared off.

"You'd better call her husband, Don," Alice said.

I telephoned Mr. Stern at work, describing what had happened in as unalarming a way as possible, but advising him to take his wife to their doctor for a sedative.

I learned later that the family doctor had referred Mrs. Stern to a psychiatrist. The psychiatrist, unfortunately, was unable to help her either. She remained agitated, nervous, irrational.

As her pastor I had failed Mrs. Stern. She had come to me for help and I had not been able to give it to her. Still, in some unexplained way I had the feeling that I was not altogether on a wrong track. The abnormal behavior that modern medicine could not help. That strange overreaction to my words about an evil spirit. The voice-change when she became agitated, sounding— well, almost like a ventriloquist speaking through the mouth of a puppet.

I felt that I had been on the verge of discovering something real and life-changing—when as usual I had blown it by my own clumsiness. What on earth had made me mention to that unsuspecting lady the direction my own private thinking had been taking? I had forgotten that while I'd been researching and pondering this whole weird realm, Mrs. Stern had not. No wonder I had nearly scared her out of her wits!

Had I known then that I was destined to see precisely the same irrational symptoms repeated many times over in people who were at the point of receiving dramatic and effective help, I might have felt less discouraged by this initial failure. At the time, however, I could only see that my approach had catapulted Mrs. Stern into a psychotic reaction and brought acute embarrassment to me.

The whole idea of demons and demon-possession had become

utterly repulsive to me. I resolved that I would never again bring up the subject. If someone were to come to me about it—someone who believed in such things and wanted help—well, I supposed I would not dismiss the idea as automatically as I once would have. But I wasn't going to wish any such hobgoblin stuff on innocent people.

And the chances of anyone in this day and age asking me to cast out a demon, I reflected reassuringly, were about as likely as a visit from the court jester.

It was the following week that I was invited to speak in a small town just west of Pittsburgh. I drove the seventy miles on a beautiful sunlit Sunday afternoon, twisting my way through the picturesque hills and valleys of western Pennsylvania. The church was located on a quiet street lined with elm trees. I pulled into the churchyard in the closing-in dusk, fed by the beauty of the scene. A simple white-frame church stood against a backdrop of trees. Soft lights shone welcome through the window arches and the tall steeple seemed to beckon people to look up and see God.

I introduced myself to the pastor and we chatted on the church steps as additional cars pulled into the parking lot. Soon we were joined by a rough-hewn man with a thatch of gray hair that looked as if it had not been combed all day, and a woman in a flowered print dress. My host introduced us. This was Brother Dawson and his wife, Stella. Brother Dawson was pastor of a country church nearby. He was to share the platform with me that evening.

The hour for the service arrived and I took my place next to Brother Dawson. I was reviewing the things I wanted to say when somewhere between the hymn singing and the announcements, Brother Dawson leaned toward me. He probably meant to speak in a whisper, but his voice was loud enough to be heard twelve pews back.

"We have a man here tonight who is possessed with demons and we want you to pray for him."

If someone had thrown a pitcher of ice water in my face I couldn't have been more startled. Here were jester, minstrels, knights in armor—the whole medieval panorama.

"Is that right?" I murmured, staring straight ahead and trying to sound as if I received a dozen such requests each week. Actually I was in a panic as I remembered Mrs. Stern; I had visions of trying to corral a wild man running all over the church.

It was difficult to keep my mind on the service after that. At the close we prayed and counseled with the people seeking help until only five of us were left: the pastor; gray-haired Brother Dawson; his wife, Stella; myself; and—the man who was "possessed." I studied him covertly. He was a wizened little fellow, probably in his late fifties. Rheumy eyes blinked nervously in a sallow face. What in the world had I got into!

The pastor suggested we go down to a prayer room in the church basement. It was empty and cold. The floor was rugless nor were there curtains at the windows high in the walls, so that words had a hollow ring. The group turned to me.

"Shall we begin?" my host said.

What was I supposed to do now?

I bowed my head and we stood there in silence. I did not want to tell these good people how little I knew about this kind of ministry, for fear of undermining their faith. I winced inwardly as I felt their eyes on me in innocent confidence: I was the important guest speaker from out of town, the seminary graduate, the spiritual expert.

I closed my eyes. "Lord Jesus," I breathed silently, "protect these children of yours from any mistakes I may make."

"Shall we begin?" the pastor said again.

I motioned to the little man to sit down. He was shaking. I knew how he felt.

Trying to appear calmer than I was, I told the man to relax, that we were there to help him, that he need not be afraid. "You believe God can help you, don't you?"

He nodded nervously. "I guess so, b-but what are you going to do?"

"You want to get rid of them things tormenting you, don't you Sam?" Brother Dawson said, putting his huge hand on Sam's shoulder.

Sam lowered his head. "Yes, I do."

"Go ahead, Brother Basham."

Desperately, I tried to recall what I had read in the Bible about such moments. "What seems to be Sam's difficulty?" I asked, stalling.

Standing behind Sam, Brother Dawson tapped his own forehead with his finger. "He can't remember anything. We just got Sam out of the county hospital two weeks ago." I cringed at the news. That's all I need, I thought, a real mental case.

"He thinks he's losing his marbles," Brother Dawson went on. "Stella and me, we been trying to teach him Scriptures, but when we ask him to say them back his mind just goes blank."

"That's right," Sam interrupted, his eyes blinking owlishly. "My mind goes blank—just goes blank!"

Dawson went on to say that Sam himself thought he was bound by evil spirits. "That's what you said, right Sam?" He clapped Sam on the shoulder. Sam said that was right. "So we brought you here to be delivered, right Sam?"

Sam's face crumpled and he began to whimper, ". . . just goes blank."

Dawson stepped aside and once again all eyes turned to me.

Still fighting panic, I asked aloud for Jesus to protect us in all that we were about to do. Then I remembered something. Before dealing with the lunatic man in Gadara, Jesus had commanded the spirit troubling him to give its name.

"According to the Bible," I said, "evil spirits have names. Deaf spirit, dumb spirit, Legion . . . names like that." I also recalled the sentence, "With authority he commands the unclean spirits . . . ," so I determined to sound authoritative. I should have warned Sam first, but feeling both foolish and desperate I leaned over him and in a loud voice cried out:

"By the authority of Jesus Christ, I command you to give your name!"

Sam's reaction was immediate. He jumped high in his chair and let out a shriek.

"Sam Jenkins!" he shouted. "That's my name, Sam Jenkins!"

Brother Dawson's gentle eyes twinkled. "Well, he remembered his name anyhow."

Hoping I didn't look as idiotic as I felt, I apologized. "No Sam, you don't understand. I wasn't speaking to you, I was speaking to those . . . to that . . ." I couldn't bring myself to say it. "I was speaking to that thing tormenting you. Don't you see?"

"You mean the demon?"

"Yes, Sam. I mean the . . . er . . . demon. We want to find out what it is. Now let's try again, okay?

"You spirit tormenting Sam," I said in a softer voice, "by the authority of Jesus Christ, I command you to tell me who you are!"

Sam screwed up his face. "Forgetfulness."

I looked at the pastor. "Forgetfulness?" I echoed.

The pastor nodded encouragingly.

I took another deep breath, then plunged ahead. "All right, you spirit of forgetfulness, I command you in the name of Jesus to come out of Sam!"

Sam shuddered slightly and sighed.

I watched him carefully for a moment, but nothing else happened.

"Think it came out, Sam?" Brother Dawson asked.

Sam opened his eyes. He seemed a little calmer. "I don't know. Maybe."

"Let's try again," I said. I repeated the command. Once again Sam seemed to give an involuntary, mild shudder. Was anything really happening? One more time I ordered the spirit of forgetfulness to leave.

Sam trembled again, more violently this time. For several seconds it seemed as if he were having some kind of seizure. Just as I began to be frightened, the shaking stopped.

And then I saw something which amazed me, and which completely changed the mood of the scene there in that echoing basement prayer room. For an invisible mask seemed to slip from Sam's face and some lurking—did I dare say "presence"—behind his eyes seemed to melt away. It's hard to put into words exactly how Sam changed. It was as if he had been wearing spectacles which distorted the way he really looked. Those spectacles were now removed. Sam *looked* different. With a shy smile he glanced up at the Dawsons. For the very first time I began to wonder if this were more than a meaningless performance. I had been acting in imitation of certain biblical events, but deep within me where my most honest self lives, I'd been doubtful and afraid that I was trespassing on a province that had best be left to the mystics and the powerful.

And then the thing happened which undid me altogether. For Sam began to speak.

"Bless the Lord, O my soul, and all that is within me bless His Holy name. Bless the Lord, O my soul and forget not all His benefits, Who forgiveth all thy sins and healeth all thy diseases . . . ."

On and on in a quiet voice, Sam continued to quote Scripture.

"Those are the Bible verses we've been teaching him!" Stella said. "He's never been able to repeat a one."

For the next several minutes we listened in wonder as Sam recited passage after passage. Tears were flowing down his cheeks. There were some on mine too.

"Thank God," Dawson said very softly. "Oh, thank God."

I was amazed. It was awesome. I felt ten feet tall.

As we made our way out of the church Sam edged over to me and gripped my hand. He looked younger.

"Thank you, Brother Basham," he said. "You must have great faith to be able to do that."

"No, Sam," I replied, "if you want to know the truth I was just as frightened as you were. But we can thank God for what He has done for you tonight."

"Yes," Sam nodded. Then, almost parenthetically, he added, "You know, for years I've been hearing a strange voice. In fact, it kept yammering at me all the way here tonight. 'You go to that meeting and you'll die!' it said. Over and over it kept saying that. That's why I was so scared!"

Then he smiled. "But the devil always was a liar, wasn't he?"

On the drive back to Sharon I had plenty to think about. As I considered the strange series of events which had been battering and shaping my ministry since the days of those powerful prayer meetings in Toronto I could not shake the feeling that this night's experience was the most crucial of all.

Yet on the other hand, the bizarre incident I had just been through seemed almost too far out to believe. Couldn't what happened to Sam be explained psychologically? Couldn't my authoritative "role playing" have given him a chance to bring to the surface and shake off some early trauma, some carry-over from childhood? How could anyone in his right mind, in the twentieth century, believe that we had actually dislodged from Sam's personality some alien, evil, spiritual entity?

But then, I reminded myself, I had agreed for the time being to leave the preconceptions of this century out of it. For the present I was applying the scientific method: observe first, try to fit your observations into a system of thought later. And— I had to confess—taking the Bible at its literal word had produced results. There had been a change in Sam, a change for the better. There was no arguing that. I fell into bed that night with the first glimmer of hope I had had about this whole strange business.

And promptly forgot my own hard-earned lesson. I had been invited to lead a house prayer meeting in nearby Ohio. Without remembering the disastrous consequences of springing this topic, unprepared, on Mrs. Stern, I launched into a description of the experience with Sam Jenkins. Icily, my hostess interrupted.

"I never let myself think about loathsome things like Satan and evil spirits," she said. "I keep my thoughts on Jesus."

"What's so loathsome about a man being set free from torment?" I began—then recalled, too late, how many weeks had passed before I could take even the halfway objective view I now tried to assume toward such things. "Perhaps I did make the incident sound a bit dramatic," I apologized. "Nevertheless, it happened just the way I told it."

But the lady was not buying. "We invited you here," she scolded, "to talk about the gifts of the Holy Spirit and the wonderful *clean* things that have been happening in your church. We had no idea you were mixed up in anything so far out. It strikes me that your friend Sam Jenkins—or someone—is suffering from overactive imagination."

There was no mistaking, from her tone, whose imagination she meant.

"Basham," I asked myself as I climbed into my car two strained and unproductive hours later, "when are you going to learn to keep your big mouth shut?" Do not, I drilled myself all the way home, do not *ever* initiate this topic! Wait for people to come to you, if they're going to. If God wants you to find out more about this area, He'll send situations your way. But don't go out looking for trouble!

And the very next week it seemed to me that such a situation did present itself. A woman who attended another church in Sharon phoned to ask if she could come in for a consultation. Over the telephone she described her difficulties with a violent and abusive husband.

The next morning she came to my office at the church and spent a long hour telling me the details of her trouble. "I feel so hounded," she concluded sadly. "I sometimes wonder if my husband doesn't have a . . . a *demon* or something, he's so cruel!"

My heart skipped a beat. Could God be offering me another opportunity to experiment with biblical tools? Much too quickly I plunged into a description of the authority the first disciples had assumed in Jesus' name over evil spirits.

"I don't know what you mean," the woman said.

"I mean the spirit of violence in your husband."

The woman got up out of her chair, eyes fixed warily on mine. "You sound like someone from the Middle Ages," she said. "Are you sure you know what you're talking about?"

I felt my face flush. No, I wasn't at all sure. Certainly I should have approached the subject more slowly. Instead, I compounded one mistake with another. "But *you,*" I said defensively, "are the one who brought up the subject of demons."

"Oh, that! That was just a—a figure of speech. I didn't mean for you to take it literally." She sat down again. "Can't you just pray for me? I came here for strength." Reaching into her purse she drew cut a handkerchief and pressed it to her cheek.

Realizing I'd fumbled the ball once again, I reverted to the role of consoling pastor, listened to her troubles for another half-hour and ended by saying a long and probably ineffectual prayer about them. At the close, though, she seemed relieved. She smiled, patted me on the hand, and stood up.

"Thank you for listening to all my problems, and for the prayer. I feel much better now." She had one hand on the knob when she paused.

"You know, you really frightened me when you began talking about—" she gave a little shudder "—evil spirits." Then she laughed. "But this persecution from my husband, it's very real you know. It's not just some imaginary demon or something." She sighed. "But that prayer was just beautiful. You ministers are *such* a comfort."

I saw her to the outside door, then returned to my office and slumped down at my desk. Right then I couldn't care less whether evil spirits were imaginary or not. I was thoroughly disenchanted with the whole unwelcome subject that seemed to bring me nothing but awkwardness and embarrassment.

From now on I would concentrate on the positive aspects of Christianity. I'd forget the entire distasteful topic of Satan and evil powers, and get back to working on my book manuscript. It seemed a much safer endeavor. I didn't realize that this very decision would prove a big factor in launching me toward precisely the area I wanted to avoid.

6

Face Up with a Miracle

I HAD been working on the book—off and on—for over three years. Now I started on it once again, stealing hours of companionship from Alice and the children to bury myself behind the typewriter. But somehow, what I produced seemed singularly inadequate. I doubted if what I was writing was good enough to be published, and those doubts seemed to chase me through every page I typed.

Still I kept at it, knowing even as I did that one of my motives was fear. I was counting on possible income from a book to help solve the spiraling financial problems Alice and I faced. Every month our bills mounted higher, and with each new money crisis the pressure grew stronger to complete the manuscript.

Naturally, then, any problems with it were doubly threatening. And I was having real problems. The nearer the book drew to completion, the more dissatisfied I became with it. The stories were all true, but they didn't sound true. I polished and repolished, but nothing helped. I would lay it aside for days, then come back and examine it to see if I could detect what was wrong. The account of our spiritual discoveries was factual enough but somehow it just wasn't us.

68

One morning during my 5:00 o'clock prayer time I asked God either to show me what was wrong or else let me give up the manuscript altogether. Almost instantly a strange thought dropped into my mind.

"Write it all!"

The words were so unexpected that I stumbled over them. Hadn't I covered all the material I was supposed to cover? But the thought remained so vivid that I got out my last version and read it straight through. Bit by bit I began to see what "Write it all!" meant.

I had told only half a story. I had shared the spiritual victories but not the struggles which surrounded them. I had shown the mountain peaks but not the valleys which joined them. No wonder the landscape looked distorted.

"Write it all!" In the weeks that followed I did just that, slowly reshaping the narrative, showing our family in far less heroic proportions. But at least the book was honest. And indeed the spiritual victories seemed even more striking against a background of stress.

Satisfied at last that I was on the right track I began to submit outlines and sample chapters to publishers. Sometimes it seemed that the query had hardly hit the bottom of the mail drop before the form rejection was back in my own stamped self-addressed envelope:

We regret that your manuscript does not meet our editorial needs at this time.

With each rejection I grew glummer. My early doubts had been right—the manuscript was worthless. And then, just as I was about to throw the whole thing in the incinerator, and the typewriter after it, a letter came from a small publisher in California. He liked it: when could he see the completed manuscript?

Now I worked day and night, running from my desk to the mailbox as each chapter was finished. *Face Up with a Miracle* was published in the summer of 1967. First sales were doubtless modest by established writers' standards, but hugely encouraging to me. Reactions by phone and letter were favorable too. Of course many of these came from friends, but as the response continued to grow I began to realize that in spite of its faults, the book seemed to be proving a real help to people. I also began to glimpse the influence of the written word, finding with some amusement that people are impressed with an "author." With a book behind me I seemed to become, overnight, something of an authority on the Christian life.

"Did you know your husband is becoming a minor celebrity?" I teased Alice one day. "See that you treat him accordingly." And I handed her a letter inviting me to address a ministers' meeting in a nearby city. I did not yet realize what problems such invitations were to create.

Another surprise was the attitude of readers of the book toward me and my family. Perfect strangers would walk up and begin chatting with Alice and me as though we were long-lost cousins, asking us personal questions and sharing their own experiences. Taken aback at first, we soon realized that they had identified personally with our story. Now I saw the wisdom in having had to rewrite the book, fears, failures, and all. People saw themselves in these things.

Perhaps the most gratifying response came from the letters. Soon we were receiving a small but constant stream of mail from ministers, missionaries, businessmen, housewives, and students all across the United States; some even from Europe and Asia. Something melted inside as I realized that by means of the book, my ministry had suddenly been extended halfway around the world.

But while the book brought such large satisfactions, it also created problems. During my ministry at East Side Church I had tried to teach the spiritual principles which the incidents in the book illustrated, but with little effect on most of the congregation. Honest, hardworking people, most seemed content with church life as they had always known it and did not share my concern for spiritual renewal.

The book made our differences harder to sweep under the carpet. True, some parishioners who had not been impressed by what they heard became interested by what they read, and we began to see new faces in the midweek prayer meeting. But the reaction of the majority was not so positive. They felt the testimony of the book was "too personal" and "too emotional."

And invitations to speak kept coming. At first grateful for the opportunity to share with other churches nearby, I wondered what to do as invitations to more distant places began to arrive.

Three months after the book was published I was asked to attend a four-day convention in New York City, one featuring my book in its literature booth. I had one week of vacation time remaining; the church board agreed I could use it for the trip to New York. Those attending the convention were receptive to my ministry and the few days there seemed as spiritually rewarding as a whole year in my own church. It was a heady, intoxicating experience.

Returning home I faced the fact that it was also the last such excursion. From now on I would have to limit my outside speaking engagements to those which required only a half-day or evening of my time. Some church members always murmur when the preacher ministers out of town—and who has a better right to an opinion than those who pay his salary! Yet the invitations continued to come in.

One day I found myself thinking, "If only I were not serving a pastorate, I could accept every one of these!" As soon as I said it I knew it was just wishful thinking. How could I possibly leave the work I had been in for over fifteen years? Begin a new life at the age of forty-one, with my wife and five children to support? The very idea was ridiculous!

But the more my mind rejected it, the more the idea persisted. How would it feel to be free from the endless detail of administration and committee meetings? Free to concentrate all my energies on the kind of ministry I felt was most important? Free to speak only to audiences ready to hear what I had to share? It sounded exciting . . . and impossible.

How would we live? Theoretically there would be some money in royalties from the book and some honorariums from speaking engagements, but these two sources would be totally inadequate. Even as it was—with a salary coming in each month, an expense allowance, and a parsonage provided—the unpaid bills were increasing. Hadn't I had enough sleepless nights over money troubles?

And each time I reached this point in my reasoning, I would hear another voice, a prodding inner voice that seemed to say: Trust Him. Throw yourself and your family with complete abandon upon God. Commit yourself totally to a life of faith. Ministers and missionaries had done it before, and the testimony of their lives had inspired millions. Could I do it? More to the point, would I really be stepping into total dependency upon God, or merely making a foolish attempt to escape the responsibilities inherent in any career?

What about my obligation to the church I was serving? We were in the process of adding that educational wing to our church. The congregational meeting was coming up to vote on the architect's proposal. Ours was a busy, thriving church and I was heavily occupied with the duties every minister is trained for and expected to discharge.

Not only that, my family was content in Sharon. We had a lovely home in a fine neighborhood. The children were happy in school and we had carved a comfortable and useful niche for ourselves in the life of the community. True, I had written a book which had provided some additional preaching opportunities. But give up my career? Uproot my family and become some kind of itinerant evangelist with no parish of my own and no real assurance that my family would be provided for?

No, the more I considered the risks, the more attractive life in the pastorate appeared. There was no need to do anything foolish or impractical. I could continue to minister right here in Sharon, accepting an occasional invitation to speak outside. It was a compromise, but then, all life is a compromise.

Over the following weeks, I turned down most of the invitations which came in. Those I did accept were a joy to my heart. Whereas the East Side people often resisted talk about healing and the gifts of the Holy Spirit, the opposite was true away from home. Gradually I discovered that the arrangement which sounded so logical was giving me no peace. As I continued to try and balance the two ministries week after week, what I had hoped would be the best of two possible worlds simply brought frustration. It took a shove from the Lord to get me off dead center—and the shove was in the direction I least expected.

One Sunday night I was invited to preach at the Newcastle Revival Center in Newcastle, Pennsylvania. At the close of the service, the pastor of the church, Mrs. Virginia Bright, requested Alice and me to kneel at the altar so that the congregation could pray for us as they often did for visitors. A small group gathered behind us, some laying hands on our shoulders. And then I heard Mrs. Bright's voice, close to my ear.

"The Lord shows me that you will be greatly used in a ministry of deliverance, discerning and casting out evil spirits."

My heart nearly stopped beating in my chest. It was months

since I had given a thought to the whole ugly realm of Satan and demons. And certainly Virginia Bright had no knowledge of my former interest in those spooky matters.

Then, as we were preparing to leave the church, a stranger came up to me. He could not have heard Virginia's prophecy and certainly *he* had no information about me whatever. I'd never seen the man before. Yet as he shook my hand he said, "Mr. Basham, I have just had a vision in which I saw you speaking in a large assembly hall, many times larger than this one. It was filled with hundreds of people and you were telling them of the mighty authority Christians have in the name of Jesus. Then I saw you commanding evil spirits to come out and many people being set free."

I was too stunned to speak. Before I could even find out who he was, the stranger had walked away.

As Alice and I drove back to Sharon, my mind went back to the embarrassing scenes when I had tried to deliver people who did not want deliverance, or when I'd brought up the subject only to have a roomful of people turn away.

"I thought, with the way things have been going since the book was published, that all that weird stuff about demons was behind us," I grumbled. "I thought I had it all settled about my ministry."

"Honey," Alice's voice was gentle but sober, "I'm not sure God led you through all He did—including your experience with Sam Jenkins—just to let you forget all about it. And I'm not sure it's wise to try and shut the doors the Lord opens for you."

Deep inside I knew what Alice said was true. There was something there, all right, something poorly understood and long overlooked by the church. *Someone* was going to have to look into it one of these days, I felt sure of that. Just as long as it wasn't me.

So the Lord had to shove a little harder, and this time the results proved to be drastic.

The congregational meeting was coming up in one week. I had planned a special service and sermon to fit the occasion. It seemed certain that the recommendation of the building committee would pass and that we would soon be launched in the actual work of erecting our new building.

The service itself flowed smoothly enough. There were smiles of approval throughout the congregation as I challenged every member to commit himself. At the close of the service the chairman of the building committee called the congregation to order and a spokesman gave the architect's proposal, using a large colored rendering of the proposed building to good effect. Standing at the back of the church watching the proceedings I knew I was playing the professional minister's role to the hilt, encouraging the building of bigger buildings to house more effective committees to build bigger buildings with. But with my decision to stick to the pastorate, I knew I had to live with this way of doing things.

"Mr. Chairman!" A committee member was on his feet to make a motion. "Mr. Chairman, I move that the congregation accept the program as outlined."

Another member of the committee quickly seconded the motion. Then several influential members of the congregation rose to express their unqualified support. The whole meeting was proceeding smoothly toward its intended objective.

"Mr. Chairman, I have something I want to say." Ward Weatherby walked to the front of the church. "Most of you already know my sentiments about this building program," he began. "I have been a hundred percent in favor of it from the beginning. Nevertheless I feel I must ask everyone here to vote *against* this proposal."

He paused as people glanced wonderingly at one another.

"I feel we should vote against this motion," Ward continued, "not because I'm against the building program but because I am deeply concerned about a matter vital to our church's welfare. I feel the time has come to decide whether we are to continue in the proven traditions of our denomination, or whether we are to follow the raw enthusiasms of our minister. To me, this baptism in the Holy Spirit, this talk about miracles, these prayer meetings where you babble in some kind of gibberish, all smack of fanaticism. I'm so concerned about this that I'm asking all of you to vote down the building proposal and—while the whole congregation is still together—to discuss the direction our church is taking. That's all I have to say."

He had said enough. Our carefully planned congregational meeting fell apart. Everywhere people were speaking at once. One man jumped to his feet. "Whatever we decide, we must not let it split the church! We must remain united. We must remain *calm!*" He sounded anything but calm.

Next, a woman walked rapidly to the front of the church. My heart sank. A troubled lady who had found a measure of help in our prayer meetings, she was highly emotional and given to tearful outbursts. Turning to face the pews she began to defend my work; but after a half-dozen sentences she broke down and began to cry incoherently. She wailed her way back to her seat.

As others rose to comment, it suddenly seemed as if I were viewing the whole unpleasant proceedings from far off. A kind of overwhelming sadness came over me. I sensed that God was showing me my future if I stayed in the pastoral ministry: there would be many many meetings like this one. I could foresee either years of compromised witness as I struggled to play the ministerial game, or angry, divided congregations learning love neither of God or neighbor if I persisted according to my own lights.

"Lord," I whispered, "I do see. I ask You to forgive me for clinging to this job out of fear—financial, social, whatever. If You will not let the church be torn apart over this incident, I promise that I will trust You. I will follow You wherever You lead."

I walked to the front of the church and with a strange peace faced the congregation.

"I appreciate Ward Weatherby's concern and I am not surprised at his reaction. We have somewhat differing views on the mission of the church, Ward and I. But this meeting was not called to discuss our spiritual life. It was called for one purpose only, to vote on the building committee's proposal. I request that we confine our discussion to the matter at hand."

I sat down and immediately the chairman put the question to a vote. The motion was carried. The crisis was past. The building program was saved. Two days later I announced my resignation, effective in six weeks' time.

7

The School of Faith

IT IS difficult to describe the way I felt after notifying the church board of my decision to leave the pastorate.

Excitement, expectancy, near panic—all were there.

On the night of the day I made my announcement I slept very little. Not so Alice: she seemed strangely and wonderfully at peace about the decision. But I turned restlessly on the bed, hearing a distant clock tell the hours, returning again and again to the central question: how would my family live?

One morning four weeks before the resignation date I had set, my friend Bill Bair asked me to have lunch with him. Bill had taken the step I was now taking, having quit an excellent job with the People's Gas and Electric Company in Pennsylvania in order to devote full time to the work of placing troubled youngsters in Christian foster homes. After we had placed our orders, Bill leaned across the table and looked me in the eye.

"Don," he said, "I believe the Lord is telling me you're to work with us. We need someone to serve as a kind of roving ambassador, to move about the country and share our vision. We will pay you the same salary you're receiving at East Side and furnish you with a home and a car allowance. You'll be free to travel and speak anywhere you feel led to go."

Bill leaned back in his chair. "Well, what do you think?"

I had only one reaction: hooray! "Bill, it sounds great and the timing is almost unbelievable! Here I give up security one day and have it offered back the next on my own terms." Not wanting to sound too eager I added, "I'll talk it over with Alice and we'll let you know for sure tomorrow."

But to my astonishment Alice, when I had relayed the good news, looked more puzzled than delighted. "It's generous of him," she admitted, "but—but, Don, is this what you're leaving the pastorate to do? To get involved with another organization?"

Sobered by her question, I began to give the matter a second look. And the more I thought about it, the more I prayed about it, the sharper the conviction became that this was not God's direction for us. Reluctantly, I telephoned Bill and told him we could not accept. "I don't know why either—except I keep getting the feeling that I'm not supposed to be tied down."

"We don't want to tie you down, Don. We only want you to tell our story. How about working for us part time?"

Bill was a hard man to say no to. And after all, in a month we'd have no place to live.

"How about this," I said. "I'll be your representative part time and you can help underwrite the cost of our renting a house. Say—a hundred and fifty a month." After all, I rationalized, for years our home had been furnished by the churches where we served.

"Fine!" Bill replied. "Starting next month you'll receive a monthly check for one hundred and fifty dollars. We're glad to have you with us."

Meanwhile we faced another decision: *where* were we going to live? In theory, if my chief work was to be speaking and writing, home base could be anywhere at all. "New England!" was Alice's vote. "I've always wanted to live there!"

"It's my favorite part of the country too," I said, "but—are we going where we want or where God wants?"

"Where He wants, of course. But how do we find out?"

We were both silent for a moment as though the name of a state and a city might ring from the air. "Well," I said, "we ask for guidance. We see where the invitations to speak are coming from. We see where the book's being read."

And so over the next two weeks I kept a geographical record of every letter and phone call on these matters. When I tallied them up, I could hardly believe it. Though I had spoken recently in many different parts of the country, over half the mail and a third of the phone calls came from a single state.

"Florida!" said Alice when I showed her the result of my little poll. "Oh, Don, I couldn't! Bugs and heat and sand and—"

"And elderly ladies sitting around in rocking chairs," I added my own stereotype of the place. "But look at this. An order for fifty copies of the book from Fort Lauderdale. Ten to a bookstore in Miami, six to Fort Pierce. Only twelve other book orders from the whole rest of the country. Six requests to speak, four of them in Florida! Orlando, Tallahassee, Miami, and West Palm Beach." I dropped the letters one by one on the kitchen table.

Alice stared at them, then turned back to the sink. "No fall colors," she said.

I kept two of the Florida dates the following week and came home with a different outlook on the state. "I take it back about the rocking chairs," I told Alice. "I've never met so many young people in my life!"

In addition, the elder of a Presbyterian church where I had spoken (admittedly the man was in real estate) had given me a brochure showing that Florida had the lowest cost-of-living in the nation. "No heating bills," I pointed out. "No winter clothes." Seven winter coats—how much would we save right there? "Also, honey, have you thought what a New England winter would be like with me traveling? Until Glenn's older, who's going to put the chains on the car?"

Alice looked far from convinced. And then, within a week after I entered into the part-time arrangement with Bill Bair, the telephone rang. It was our friends Nelson and Sue Makinson, with an incredibly generous suggestion. God had prompted them, they said, to offer us their home for just enough to meet their payments on it. Where was the house? Pompano Beach, Florida. And what were the monthly expenses? A hundred and fifty dollars.

In the face of guidance like this, Alice's visions of flies and cockroaches began to waver. We gratefully accepted the Makinsons' offer and began giving away sleds and snowsuits.

Above all, I yearned to be able to leave Sharon free of debt. Since my last visit to the bank, unpaid bills, as usual, had accumulated. With the balance we still owed on our station wagon, they now totaled over $2,000. Where was I going to get that kind of money? The only asset I had in the world was the church pension fund into which I'd mailed dimes and dollars as often as I could—and I certainly wasn't going to dip into that! Alice and I were counting on that for our retirement.

It was while I was adding figures at my desk one morning that the ridiculousness of the situation swept over me. Here we were, preparing to cast ourselves on God for our every need—and I was prudently squirreling away a little cash for our old age. If He could be trusted for today, He could be trusted for tomorrow. I wrote denominational headquarters, canceling out the fund. The refund came to just over $2,000.

Now I just hoped we could *stay* free of debt. What bank would make me a loan next time! I pictured the familiar yellow application blank. *Where employed?* Not employed. *Salary?* None. *Is spouse employed?* No. *Other income?* $150 per month.

The day the movers came it snowed. Our driveway was so icy the van had to park in the street while the moving men struggled through six inches of snow on the lawn. At intervals during the day, church members dropped by to wish us well. One woman lingered at the door.

"I'm not sure how to say this," she began. "I didn't think you really believed all those things you said. But now . . . ," she glanced around at the nearly empty rooms, "I see that you really do believe. That makes a tremendous difference in, well, everything!" Her eyes began to mist; she gave Alice a big hug and stepped out into the still-falling snow.

Among the first of the neighbors we got to know in Pompano Beach was an attorney named Jack Musselman. He and his wife, Anne, had a weekly prayer meeting in their home where—though we did not suspect it then—we were to have some of the most startling experiences of our lives. But the first Thursday night we went, we were so put off by one particular woman that we almost decided not to go back.

"Sister Sadie," as she introduced herself, wore a long-sleeved black dress, plain to the point of severity, and carried a huge black Bible. Extremely tall and lean, her face was framed by strands of long, bleached hair. About halfway through the meeting Sister Sadie jumped to her feet, closed her eyes, and began to speak in a loud, wailing voice.

"Oh yes, Lord," she cried. "Yes, yes, Lord. Oh hallelujah! Yes, Lord!" Then she launched into what I suppose was meant to be a prophecy. The message had something to do with God's judgment being visited on this vile world and on the vile backsliders in the church. I was almost ashamed of my reaction, it was so negative. To me this seemed like a caricature of a genuine spiritual experience. I couldn't foresee that one day soon Sister Sadie would pose me some of the most troubling questions of my ministry.

And all the while I was in training, learning to trust God. Our only assured income was the $150 a month from the Bair Foundation. Speaking dates brought in an unpredictable amount, sometimes nothing, sometimes $25, sometimes a hundred or more. And sure enough, in March the crisis I had been expecting arrived: our bank balance reached zero. I broke the news to Alice but she only smiled as she stirred the abundant helping of rice with a tiny portion of hamburger in the skillet. "Don't you think God knows?" she said. "He'll look after us! You'll see."

I wished I could be as sure. The next morning I opened my wallet and stared in dismay at the total financial resources of the Basham family. A single ten and two lonesome one dollar bills.

Furthermore there was an immediate expenditure needed. The night before I had noticed that one of the headlights in our station wagon was burned out.

"Get the headlight replaced immediately."

I almost looked around, the voice seemed so clear. Surely my mind was playing tricks on me. But the inner impression remained. "If you had hundreds of dollars in the bank," the silent voice went on, "would you hesitate to spend three dollars on a headlight? Why not trust My bank?"

Suddenly I saw what God was doing for me: He was putting me on a tightrope over a chasm. I had not been trusting Him at all! I had been trusting that dwindling bank account.

"All right, Lord, I'll go."

So I climbed into the car, drove to the garage, and had the light replaced. I confess that I winced as I paid the mechanic his three dollars. "That leaves me only nine," I thought as I drove home.

Yet—what was this little island of peace which seemed to emerge now in the middle of my fears? Was this whole experience to teach me that taking a simple step-of-obedience would release calm assurance?

As a matter of fact the assurance was followed at once by substance. As I arrived at the house the postman turned up our walk. Among the envelopes was one from the Bair Foundation with the $150 rent check, and another from my publisher with a royalty check for $400. I grabbed Alice by the waist and swung her around in a dance of celebration.

As we went to bed that night we indeed had hundreds in the bank. But the real victory that day was not the money's arriving. The real victory was learning to obey.

Entering preparatory training in the life of faith was like enrolling in a new and different kind of school. Lovingly, but persistently, God was teaching Alice and me and the children to trust Him completely. It was the background without which He could never have led me into the fear-inspiring areas that lay ahead.

The next lesson dealt with the $150 a month I was receiving from Bill Bair. The thought began coming to me that I should represent his Foundation without pay. I finally decided that the next time I visited there I would offer to release them from their agreement. I felt sure the board of trustees would insist that I stay on the payroll. Then I would graciously give in and my conscience would be clear.

Within a month a speaking trip took me to Pennsylvania in time for their semiannual board meeting. I reported briefly on my activities for the Foundation, then modestly mentioned that I wanted to release the board from the monthly retainer. I sat down and waited to be talked out of it. To my consternation, my offer was immediately and enthusiastically accepted.

"What do I do now?" I wondered as I flew home. "How will we pay the rent?"

Sure enough when the next month's rent came due I didn't have enough to pay it. A few days later our landlord, Nelson Makinson, telephoned. "Don, I don't quite know how to say this," he began. I gripped the receiver. He was going to ask us to leave the house.

"Ever since Sue and I told you we wanted you to live in our house," Nelson went on, "we haven't felt right about the arrangement. Now we know why. It's because the Lord wants you to have the house rent free. So I'm calling to tell you that you don't owe us anything. The house is yours for as long as you want to live there."

I could scarcely believe my ears. I stammered out our thanks to Nelson, then ran to tell Alice about it. Even as I said it, though, a logical inconsistency struck me. What was the difference between our accepting $150 from the Bair Foundation, and accepting an equal dollar-value in rent-free housing?

Alice had no such problem. "It seems clear to me, dear," she said. "I think you were meddling with God's plans before. It was *your* idea to have the Foundation pay us enough to rent a house. God always intended to provide the house this way."

I was silent. Alice was right. God had moved in to upset the way I had arranged things. And He wasn't through dealing with us yet.

Next came the matter of royalties from my book. One night at a prayer meeting at the Musselmans', I seemed again to hear God's silent voice in my own spirit.

"Why do you write, Don? Is it for Me or for profit?"

The question came so unexpectedly that I was taken aback. It was true that we were receiving royalties from the book. Still, I knew that its growing success was certainly not due to any literary skill on my part, but to God's blessing on the message.

"Lord, I write for you," I answered under my breath. Immediately the thought flashed back:

"Then give up the profit."

I was completely unprepared for any such unreasonable suggestion! Those royalties represented a sizable portion of our income. Surely, I thought, it couldn't be the Lord speaking this time—it must be some neurotic voice from my own subconscious.

Then, still sitting in the Musselmans' living room, I began to recall various little incidents regarding the book. I remembered that nearly every time I traveled I would lug several dozen copies along, weighing my suitcase down until it was all I could do to lift it. I saw myself fretting and fuming about getting a book display set up in a prominent place at meetings where I spoke. At times I seemed more concerned with selling the book than I was with sharing the message it contained. I recalled one minister who ordered six copies on consignment saying he would send me the money in a week. I never heard from him again, and every time I thought of him I seethed inside.

Recalling such episodes I was ashamed at being so wrapped up with sales. No wonder the Lord had finally confronted me with it.

"All right, Lord," I sighed as the meeting was breaking up. "I'll give up the royalties."

Still it took me two days to tell Alice. To my astonishment, she was delighted.

"Worrying about book sales was hurting you," she said. "Don't you see, Don, you're free now, and the Lord is free to bless us as He chooses."

As He chooses . . . But never, until we entered this school of faith, had we dreamed how lovingly, how abundantly, how cherishingly this would be. What stunned us above all was His timing.

Unlike our plans and arrangements, His schedule was perfect. One day we were confronted with two bills which totaled $94.28—and no money to pay them. I shut myself in our bedroom the morning they arrived, determined not to come out until I had the assurance of an answer from God. The minute I started to pray, other thoughts assailed me. "If you had stayed in the pastorate where you belong, you wouldn't be in such a predicament! You'll go under for sure this time! You'll be disgraced, your family humiliated. Why don't you admit you made a mistake?"

To shut them out I opened my Bible to Philippians and read again and again the wonderful promise in chapter four: "My God shall supply all your need according to His riches in glory by Christ Jesus." After a couple of hours the burden lifted and a sense of peace seemed to fill the room. I felt God had heard and that the answer was on the way.

It arrived in the mail two days later, in the form of a letter from Ed Atkinson, a doctor friend in Greenville, Pennsylvania. We had not heard from him since leaving Sharon.

Dear Don and Alice,

It has been entirely too long since you left for Florida, leaving us in the frozen north. We have truly missed you and have wondered how things are with you. I have heard indirectly, Don, of some of your travels; that you have been in Washington and Boston. . . . The two of you are often in our prayers and if intentions were letters you would have heard from us many times before this.

Don, as we Quakers would say, your finances have been a concern on my heart. I have been busy this spring, speaking at various healing missions, and it seems they insist on giving me honorariums I don't need. So rather than refusing, I decided I knew a place where God would like them used. Therefore, please accept the two enclosed checks *as if they were honorariums for your own speaking engagements.* . . .

The two bills I had held before the Lord totaled $94.28; the two checks in Ed's letter came to $95.00.

Sometimes His timing was even more startling. I'll never forget the day shortly before Easter when once again our bank balance hovered at zero. We were sitting around the kitchen after lunch one day, Glenn and I sagely remaining silent as Cindi, Shari, Lisa, and Laura all explained to their mother why they needed new dresses. Alice listened patiently and agreed.

"But you understand, we can't always have what *we* think we need. The Lord knows what we *really* need."

"We know all that, Mother," twelve-year-old Shari burst out. "But Easter's coming! All the other kids are getting new things!"

And at that moment, of all blessed moments in the week, there was a knock at the door. Cindi answered and returned with a package from a deliveryman. Removing the outer wrapping, Alice exclaimed, "Why, it's gift-wrapped! Someone is sending us a present!"

The children crowded around her, full of curiosity. "Who's it from, Mother? What's in it?"

We all watched as Alice lifted the lid from the box. It was stuffed with nothing but tissue paper.

"Why, there's nothing in it!" Lisa exclaimed. Her blue eyes filled with tears. "Someone's playing a joke on us!"

But Lisa's disappointment was premature. At the bottom of the box was an envelope. Alice opened it, then passed it to me with a hand that trembled. It was a gift certificate on a local women's clothing store in the amount of $100.00.

"You mean we can go to that store and pick out a hundred dollars' worth of clothes?" Shari gasped. The girls began jumping up and down with delight.

"You see?" Alice's eyes were brimming too. "The Lord knew what you needed."

"But Daddy, who sent it to us?" Glenn asked. I looked again at the certificate. " 'From someone who loves you,' " I read aloud.

Five-year-old Laura nodded contentedly. "It's from God all right."

It was Easter Monday that I decided to take a walk during my 5:00 A.M. quiet time. Dawn was just beginning to break. As I headed eastward toward the brightening sky, I was aware of two very strong sensations: one was that I was almost finished with the first grade in this life of faith. And my second sensation, as I walked toward the rising sun that morning, was that the Lord had given me these lessons as a preparation for taking Him at His word.

8

Sister Sadie Objects

I WAS assisting at a week-long Bible seminar at a church in central Florida. During a question period on the fourth day, one of the slips of paper passed forward asked about the existence of demons as mentioned in the New Testament. Rather hesitantly, recalling what a volatile subject this had been in the past, I described my own Bible searching on this subject, my lone attempt to apply what I'd read with Sam Jenkins, and my feeling that there was probably more here than the church was currently paying attention to.

At the close of the session, as usual, people came forward to the altar rail for prayer. One was a tall, red-haired, sad-faced man who gave his name as Joseph P. Wheeler and said that he was confused.

"Confused?"

"All turned around. Not just now, all the time. Sometimes I get so mixed up I can't find my way home from work! You were talking about demons. Do you think I have a demon?"

Mr. Wheeler buried his head in his hands on the altar rail and my heart went out to him. I was learning to trust God in financial matters; couldn't I trust Him in other needs as well?

I bent down and whispered: "Joseph, I'm sure God knows about your confusion and I'm sure He wants to help you. You were wondering if it could be a demon. I would like you to try to name that demon."

As I spoke I laid my hand on Joseph Wheeler's head. At my touch a most remarkable thing happened. The man's hands gripped the altar rail so tight the knuckles showed white, and his whole body began to jerk. "Lord, what's happening!" I prayed silently. "Do you want me to go ahead?"

Yes, I want you to go ahead. You must not be afraid to move out in the power of the Holy Spirit.

The thought was as clear in my mind as if words had been spoken. My voice grew steadier: "Something is upsetting you! What is it, Joseph?"

"Confusion! Everything's confusion!"

I placed my other hand on his shoulder to try to quiet his shaking. "You demon of confusion," I said, "in the name of Jesus I command you to come out of this man!"

If there really was a personal devil, I thought grimly, and if he intended to scare me away from ministering to Joseph Wheeler, he was very nearly succeeding. For at these words the man lunged forward, draping himself across the altar rail so that his head almost touched the floor at my feet, and began to gag in a most unchurchly manner. Panic welled inside me. What had I done wrong?

At the same moment I became aware, all around us, of a steady murmur of prayer supporting and strengthening us. Once again a thought stood out in my mind, sovereign and distinct. *Do not be afraid. What you are seeing is Satan fighting back. You will see this many times, and it will never cease to be ugly because Satan is ugly.*

"In Jesus' name," I repeated, "I command this ugly spirit to leave!"

Joseph gave one more violent shudder and then as suddenly as it had begun, the gagging stopped. Slowly he straightened up and looked at me, eyes wide with surprise. His face, which moments before had been creased with anxiety, was as unclouded as a child's. He pressed his hands to his temples, then to the front of his head, as if feeling for something.

"It's gone!" he cried. He jumped to his feet. "It's gone! I tell you it's gone! I can think!"

In his excitement he embraced the men on either side of him. "Why—why—it's a miracle!" he stammered. "That's what it is, a miracle! Just wait till I tell my wife!"

The last I saw of him, Joseph P. Wheeler was running up the aisle toward the door of the church, still exclaiming, "Praise God! Wait'll my wife hears this!"

Mr. Wheeler's rejoicing broke up the meeting. As the last person—or so we thought—stepped through the door of the sanctuary, the minister of the church turned to me and said, "I tell you, Don, we've been praying for that man for months with no results. Now I see why. It wasn't prayer that was needed, it was authority. Somebody had to *command* that ugly thing. I can see why the Lord led you into the deliverance ministry."

"Well," I shrugged off the compliment, "it's hardly my ministry. I know very little about it."

"That certainly is the truth!"

The pastor and I whirled around. The church was not empty after all. There, a few paces away, stood a tall woman with stringy blonde hair and a glare in her eyes. I remembered her at once: it was Sister Sadie Miller who had spoken in the strange singsong at the Musselmans' prayer meeting.

"Brother Basham, I pastor a church near here and I want to ask you some questions!"

"You're welcome to ask, Sister," I began, "but I'm afraid I won't have many—"

"First I want to know why you didn't bind the evil spirit in that man before you cast it out?"

I stared at her. "Bind it? What do you mean?"

"I mean so it wouldn't go into anybody else, of course! Don't you know you were exposing everyone in this room to danger by not binding that spirit?"

I hadn't known. I hadn't even thought about it.

"And another thing. Why didn't you command the spirit to go back to the pit?"

"Well, I—"

"And how long do you fast before you attempt to cast demons out of people?"

I didn't have the slightest idea what she was talking about. "Fast?"

Sister Sadie was getting angrier. "How long do you go without eating before attempting deliverance? Don't you know Jesus told His disciples that unless they fasted, demons wouldn't come out?"

I was feeling more and more embarrassed at my obvious ignorance before this woman's expertise.

"Let me give you a word of advice, Brother," she continued, brushing the long, bleached hair from her eyes. "This is no ministry to fool around with. You have to know exactly what you're doing and observe the precautions. Demons are everywhere, you know—just watching and waiting for us to make a slip." And with an uneasy glance around the church and a final glare at me, she stalked from the building.

I was stunned. What was I letting myself in for? What kind of people went in for this "deliverance ministry"? And what dangers were involved—dangers I'd never even thought of?

"Pay no attention to Sister Sadie, Don," the minister tried to reassure me. "She's just a jealous, self-ordained woman, who heads up a small church of dissatisfied people."

But his words didn't change the fact that she had sounded sure of her facts while I was anything but sure. Every objection she had raised, apparently, was based on Scripture. It was obvious that I would have to study the Bible on this subject a lot more thoroughly.

Before I had a chance to do so, however, another challenge was flung my way. This time not from some strange, angry-eyed woman but from a man I liked and identified with.

The very next day after my encounter with Sister Sadie I flew to Washington, D.C., for a meeting with local clergymen on the subject of the charismatic movement. Apparently, interest in the subject was high for there were over thirty pastors already present in the hotel banquet room when I arrived. The organizer of the meeting, a man named Zachary Marshall, seemed delighted at the turnout. We made our way to the head table where a dignified, gray-haired man was sitting.

"This is Dr. Willard Thompson, Don," Zachary said as we shook hands. I knew Dr. Thompson by reputation. He was an elder statesman among clergymen. Beloved by a wide audience through his writings, he was to my mind a warm, deeply spiritual man. It was an honor to be sitting next to him.

The first hint that disagreement lay ahead came when Zachary leaned toward us. "I ought to let you know that Dr. Thompson has reservations about the charismatic ministry."

As we ate, the conversation turned to a well-publicized situation in which a Washington attorney had been found in a motel room with a lady who was not his wife. Although an outstanding member of the community and a regular attender at church, when he was away from home, ". . . something just seems to get hold of him," Zachary said. "It's as though some evil spirit just takes possession."

The subject of spirits seemed to be following me around! I started to say something but Dr. Thompson spoke first. He set down his coffee cup in exasperation. "Zachary, you are talking absolute nonsense! This man has his problems, yes, but he is also a fine, influential citizen. How can you say that he has an evil spirit?"

Dr. Thompson got up in annoyance and started to stroll around the room, shaking hands with most of the ministers present. It was obvious the men regarded him with the same esteem and affection I did. He did not rejoin us but sat down at a table toward the back of the room.

Zachary called the meeting to order, then introduced me. For three-quarters of an hour I shared with the ministers how the supernatural gifts of the Holy Spirit were once again reappearing in churches of all denominations. At the end I invited questions. A young Episcopal priest with a crew haircut stood up.

"Mr. Basham," he said, "I've been wondering: as you start to work in the charismatic movement, have you encountered people whose problems were caused by evil spirits?"

There it was again! I glanced toward Dr. Thompson. His face was impassive.

"Well," I said, fervently wishing the topic had not come up at this time, "I've had some experiences which puzzled me, to say the least." I drew my small New Testament from my jacket pocket and read the verse where Jesus commissions His disciples to cast out demons.

"The Scriptures have many such references, of course. Apparently churches around the country are asking themselves, is this something we should look into?" The room had grown very quiet. Feeling more uncomfortable by the minute, I described the previous day's experience with Joseph Wheeler. I also told them about Mrs. Stern's bewildering behavior and the failure of my efforts to help her. As I concluded, Dr. Thompson was on his feet.

"Now really, Mr. Basham!" his deep persuasive voice conveyed tolerance and good humor. "I confess that your interpretation of these incidents is original, but you hardly intend us to take it seriously! We all know the psychological value of prayer. And we've all encountered flighty and emotional ladies. But this talk about demons is simply archaic! I have counseled with thousands of people and not one of them, I can assure you, has been troubled by an evil spirit."

All over the room men were turning their chairs around to face the table where Dr. Thompson stood.

"Now we don't question your sincerity, Mr. Basham," he continued. "I'm sure the man you prayed for did improve. After all, the powers of suggestion are great. But most of us are not nearly so naïve as to call this—what was the word you used? 'Deliverance.' " He smiled broadly at the other clergymen and many smiled back.

"You weren't dealing with evil spirits, Mr. Basham, you were dealing with characteristics of personality, what the Bible calls carnal nature, or the old self." He pushed his chair up to the table. "I'm sorry that I must leave this gathering now, gentlemen. And I hope I haven't blunted the very admirable enthusiasm of our colleague from Florida. But I do feel it is my duty to sound a word of warning about the dangers of spiritual shortcuts. Get out your Bibles, my friends, and see what Scripture has to say about dealing with our carnal nature. That's where the real struggle lies."

Perhaps half a dozen other ministers left the room with Dr. Thompson; the question period broke up soon afterward. I flew home disgusted all over again with the whole wretched subject of demons. Once more, the very mention of them had sidetracked a discussion, got our eyes off Jesus, created dissension. Dr. Thompson needn't have worried about hurting my enthusiasm for the subject!

Indeed, except for the fact that his tone had made me feel somewhat like a small boy put in his place by the grownups, I was grateful to Dr. Thompson for his interpretation of my experiences. I devoutly hoped that he was right—hoped that we were not facing some swarming miasma of bodiless enemies, but those old problems, sin and self-will, that at least we were all familiar with. I wonder how different my thoughts would have been had I guessed the experience that lay ahead for Willard Thompson.

A few days later I came home with an armload of groceries to find Alice and the children out of the house. Here was a good opportunity to do exactly what Dr. Thompson had suggested. I set the groceries on the kitchen table (without remembering to take the ice cream out), went to my desk and brought back a Bible, a concordance, and several pads of paper. Our house was not air-conditioned, and the Florida sun beat steadily on the low roof. I took off my coat and undid my tie. With the help of the concordance I looked up every passage dealing with the carnal nature. Most of them were in the letters of Paul. I also reread all passages which mentioned "evil spirits." And the more I read the clearer it became that—to the first-century mind anyway—there was not one problem but two, and that *both* were a concern for the early church.

The old man, according to Paul, was in league with Satan and an enemy of God, but—here was the good news of the Gospel—he was put to death in Christ's own Body on the Cross.

We know that our old self was crucified with Him so that the sinful body might be destroyed and we might no longer be enslaved to sin. [Romans 6:6 RSV]

Without the crucifixion of this carnal nature, growth toward God was not possible:

> For the mind that is set on the flesh is hostile to God; it does not submit to God's law, indeed it cannot; and those who are in the flesh cannot please God. [Romans 8:7–8 RSV]

Yet Paul was also, apparently, concerned with evil spirits. The whole drama of his beating and imprisonment in Philippi, recorded in the book of Acts, resulted from his having cast a "spirit of divination" out of a young slave girl. Later, some Jewish exorcists tried to cast an evil spirit out of a man "in the name of Jesus whom Paul preaches." The spirit refused to leave, saying, "Jesus I know *and Paul I know,* but who are you?" It seemed clear that the Bible recognized two distinct categories here. On my pad I wrote:

> Scripture places both the "carnal self" and "evil spirits" within the province of Satan. The carnal self, in this view, represents an actual part of ourselves, while evil spirits are separate entities which have only taken up residence within us. Evil which is *part of us* must (by prayer and self-discipline) be put to death, or "crucified" as Paul says. Evil which is not an integral element of our nature but *has invaded us from the outside* must be evicted. This is the scriptural basis for a deliverance ministry.

I stood up and began to pace the kitchen. Two kinds of problems, two methods of dealing with them. Was it possible that Dr. Thompson was making an error of oversimplification in insisting that every difficulty he encountered in his consulting room represented a struggle with the old self?

If there really were two sources of trouble and not one, then the first job would be to determine which one we were up against. Proper diagnosis would have to precede proper treatment. I recalled vividly the time in Washington when after battling a cold for two weeks I nearly passed out in my church study one morning. To the indignant doctor who examined me I tried to defend myself.

"I've been drinking gallons of orange juice," I said. "I've taken aspirin, I've taken antihistamines, I've—"

"That's great," he said. "If this were a cold you'd probably be better. But you have pneumonia and those things don't work with pneumonia."

Had we in the church been applying the remedy for one ailment to every symptom we encountered?

The door from the carport to the kitchen flew open and the kids burst in, each with a stack of library books. Alice came last. She glanced at my page of notes, then at the grocery shopping. "Thank you, dear," she said, wiping up the puddle of what had once been butter pecan ice cream.

I put the notes away, but not the questions they had raised. If the men of the first century were right, and there was something that could bug people over and above—and quite different from —their own sinful natures, then . . . where did that leave me? Didn't it thrust me straight back into the wild-eyed world of Sister Sadie, with her paranoia about demons lurking in every corner? Wasn't this what people turned into when they dabbled in this realm?

But whatever my own revulsion, I knew I would have to take a look at her objections, too. Off and on over the next few days I tried to remember every point Sister Sadie had made.

First Sadie wanted to know why I had not bound the evil spirit in Joseph Wheeler before I commanded it to come out—so it wouldn't re-enter someone else. I checked every Scripture reference where Jesus or His disciples ministered deliverance and found not one instance of binding the spirit before casting it out. Sadie's thought probably came from Jesus' statement in Matthew 12:29 that no one can enter a strong man's house unless he first binds the strong man.

Nor could I find a single instance in which an evil spirit, cast out of one man, then entered another. In the exorcism of the possessed man whose evil spirits named themselves "Legion, for we are many," these demons—with Jesus' permission—when they had been expelled from the man, took possession of a herd of swine. But there was no record of a demon's going from one human being to another (and of course to the Jews swine were unclean animals anyhow).

Sadie felt it necessary to send demons "back to the pit." I could find no reference to Jesus or His disciples sending evil spirits to any such place, although in Luke's telling of the Legion story, the demons themselves seem to fear that Jesus will do this. "And they begged him not to command them to depart into the abyss." [Luke 8:31 RSV]

As for fasting before attempting deliverance, I found only one reference to such a discipline. When His disciples were unable to deliver a lunatic boy, Jesus chided them for their lack of faith, then added, "Howbeit, this kind goeth not out but by prayer and fasting." [Matthew 17:21] Special preparation then, by intensive prayer and fasting, was apparently required in very difficult cases. At other times the deliverance ministry seemed to be just a normal function of the Church to be accepted without drama.

"How's the research going?" Alice asked. She was standing at the stove stirring a kettle of homemade clam chowder. I had recently moved my desk to the alcove behind the kitchen counter. When we had first moved to Florida, Lisa and Laura had shared a bedroom, giving me a room to use as a study. But the girls were getting older; Lisa was seven, our "baby" Laura five, and it was time they had rooms of their own. I slipped a bookmark into the Bible and leaned back in my chair.

"Well, I've certainly seen things in the Scriptures I hadn't seen before," I replied. "Say, that chowder sure smells good—is it ready?"

Alice sampled the savory mixture. "Too much pepper. What things in the Scriptures?"

"Well, for one, why Dr. Thompson blasted me at that ministers' meeting up in Washington."

Alice poured in an additional cup of milk. "Do you know what was wrong?"

"I thought you said too much pepper."

"Not the chowder. Thompson. What was upsetting him?"

"Oh. Well, he thinks all man's problems stem from the 'old self.' A lot of Christians would agree. But the Scriptures clearly point to two separate conditions that we may have to deal with—and provide us with two sets of tools. I think God is getting the Church ready for a long-overlooked function of the Holy Spirit."

"I think it's ready now." Alice sounded thoughtful.

"Well, I don't know. Some churches may accept it, but most won't. Not yet."

"Not the Church," Alice explained patiently. "The chowder." She dipped up a steaming bowlful and set it on the counter beside me. Marveling at the inspiration which had led me to locate my desk near such a source of blessing, I picked up my spoon and dug in.

About a month after the trip to Washington Alice and I were invited by friends of the Musselmans to come and tell about our research into deliverance. At the dinner table one of the other guests mentioned that for many years he had been awakened every night with a terrible sensation of falling. Nothing he did seemed to help. He had been to psychiatrists, he'd taken pills, he'd tried to pray his way through—nothing worked. "That's exactly the kind of problem I mean," I said. "When other approaches fail, that's when I ask myself: are we up against demon activity?" Our host was aghast. He peered at me critically over the top of his glasses. "George can't have a demon," he said, "he's a Christian! How can the Spirit of God and an evil spirit be in control of the same person at the same time? You can't show me a single Scripture where a Christian has a demon!"

I returned home knowing that I needed more facts, for my friend had raised the very question that bothered me most in this whole uncanny area. Suppose for a moment there really were separate evil entities floating about the earth seeking to hurt and destroy—wouldn't Christians automatically be defended from them? Once again, while the life of the kitchen swirled around me, I buried myself in the Scriptures trying to find an answer.

But the New Testament seemed singularly indifferent to the spiritual status of people being delivered from evil spirits. Take Mary Magdalene: were the "seven demons" cast out of her before or after she became Jesus' disciple? The Bible doesn't say.

In this, as in much else, I knew I needed the counsel of someone much more experienced than I. So I picked up the phone and called Derek Prince.

Derek Prince had been a professor of logic and philosophy at Cambridge University in England. Converted to Christ while serving in the British army during World War II, he had turned his formidable scholarship to a study of the Bible. Since that time he had taught Scripture on four continents, eventually settling in the United States. I had met him once, at a seminar where we had both been speakers, and been impressed with the value he placed on deliverance. Unlike the scholarly types I had met in seminary, he not only acknowledged the reality of demons, but believed the Church had a scriptural obligation to make war on them. Since he lived in nearby Fort Lauderdale, I made an appointment to see him.

"Come in and make yourself at home!" His crisp British accent was pleasing to my ears as I stepped into his study. "I've taken the liberty of preparing a pot of tea."

He poured each of us a cup, then leaned back. "You said that you are interested in the deliverance ministry?"

I smiled apologetically. "At least," I said, "I seem to have a great many questions about it." I told Derek about the most recent one: how could a Christian be possessed by an evil spirit?

Derek sipped at his tea. "That's one of the unfortunate things about the King James Version of the Scriptures," he said. "The word which is translated in English 'possessed,' in the original Greek simply means 'to *have* a demon.' 'Afflicted' by a demon is closer to it. 'Possessed' implies ownership, as if the spirit controlled the entire person, which is a much stronger idea than the Greek implies.

"You will notice that people in the New Testament who were delivered of demons were apparently ordinary folk living ordinary lives, but who had some particular problem. One had an 'unclean spirit'—probably a struggle with lust. Another was crippled by a 'spirit of infirmity'; another a 'deaf spirit'; another a 'blind spirit.' But the afflicted person apparently functioned normally in other ways."

He picked up the teapot and refilled my cup. "I find the same thing today. People in need of deliverance have some problem area that they have not been able to surmount by other means. They may be suffering some form of mental anguish, or some inflaming physical appetite—but they are not 'possessed' by it. In fact, in other ways they may be exceptionally strong individuals."

"And these—ah, afflicted—people can be Christians?" I asked. "I don't find the Scriptures very clear on this point."

"They're not very—and many's the time I've wished they were. Scripture makes no categorical statement on the matter—neither that a Christian can, nor that a Christian can't, have an evil spirit. Although in the list of gifts in First Corinthians—why would God give His Church 'discerning of spirits' if unwelcome spirits were never going to be a problem in the Church?"

He pushed back his chair and began to walk up and down the room. "But the point, Don, is not what I theorize but what I

see. I'd estimate ninety-five percent of the people whom I have
watched receive genuine, lasting deliverance are sincere, believing
Christians—before their deliverance as well as after. Let me tell
you about my own deliverance."

My reaction must have shown on my face, because Derek
chuckled. "People often look surprised when I admit to having
harbored a demon—as though it made me a kind of second-class
Christian. But think about that for a minute. I'd far rather discover that my filthy temper—that was my particular curse—was
an invasion from outside than have it turn out to be the real me."

Derek resumed his pacing of the room. For as long as he could
remember, he said, he had been subject to terrible fits of anger.
Once as a youngster he was playing with a ball when another boy
snatched it out of his hand. A blind, unreasoning fury swept over
him. Hardly knowing what he was doing, he began to punch the
other child. "If some other boys hadn't pulled me away, I don't
know what would have happened."

When Derek became a Christian he assumed that he would be
enabled to rise above these mindless rages. But to his dismay they
remained as troublesome as ever. It was as if this one area had
in no way submitted to the Christ who was supposedly Lord of
his whole life.

"And then one day the Holy Spirit suggested to me that it
didn't have to be this way. How can I express it? It was as if I
became aware for the first time of a kind of 'presence' within my
chest. I went off by myself to pray. First I confessed my own role
in the anger as sin—tried to recall those times when I had deliberately allowed myself to become angry or nursed an anger—
and asked God to forgive me. Then I said, 'Lord, if there is anything else in me, anything that doesn't acknowledge Your king-
ship, I don't want to give it house room. I want it out.'

"I can only express what happened this way: it was as if some
heaviness, some weight, was dislodged from inside my chest

cavity and passed out through my mouth. I distinctly felt *something* leave. I didn't have any idea then what was happening. But from that day to this I have not had a single experience with the kind of irrational anger I'm talking about."

"It was a—a sort of healing?" I asked.

Derek smiled. "Funny, isn't it, how much we'd rather be 'healed' than 'delivered.' People seem to forget that—in principle anyway—it should be just as impossible for a Christian to be sick or injured as to be plagued by a demon. How can illness exist in the same body with Perfect Health? How can brokenness exist side by side with Wholeness? Theoretically, of course, they can't. And yet we experience every day that they do. When a flu bug enters my body I don't for that reason feel less a Christian. Why should I when a demon enters?

"Now the fact is, Christ has power over that flu bug. The Church has been rediscovering His healing ministry over the past decades—those parts of the Church that had forgotten—and we've seen the marvelous results. We've seen also that healing doesn't come automatically the minute we become Christians. The power becomes available, but we have to appropriate it. We have to claim it for our specific needs or it doesn't help us.

"It's exactly the same with evil spirits. It's true that they were defeated on the Cross. It's true they have no legal ground in anyone who belongs to Christ. They know it, even if we don't! But that's just what they count on—that we don't know it. They're not going to get up meekly and leave the moment we're converted. We have to *use* our authority, and this is what the Church is just now, here and there, beginning to discover."

Derek glanced at his watch and I jumped guiltily to my feet. "Thank you for sharing so much with me," I said. "It does make a kind of sense, what you just said. It's exactly how they would behave if . . ."

"If?"

I grimaced at my own predicament. "Derek, I owe you an apology. You see, I'm not even convinced these darn things exist. Here I'm taking your time with a lot of theological niceties, when I don't have the basic question answered."

"It's how evil spirits would behave, you started to say, if such improbable beings existed."

"Precisely."

Derek had begun gathering up the tea things. "That is something that only experience can settle," he said. "And I'm not sure," he added ruefully, "that it's experience which I can in all charity wish upon you."

9

Cleveland, Ohio

WHETHER he wished it or not, however, Derek's words proved prophetic. Less than a month after that discussion, I was in Cleveland taking part in a Spiritual Life Conference at which the other speaker was the Reverend H. A. Maxwell Whyte of Toronto, Canada. I knew Maxwell Whyte slightly, having met him while I was pastoring in Toronto myself. But I had had no idea, in those days, of the nature of his ministry. Indeed, if I had, I would doubtless have dismissed him as some kind of religious crank. Now, to my astonishment, I saw in the conference program that he was scheduled to speak, the second afternoon, on the topic of deliverance! While I had been gingerly getting my feet wet in these matters, Maxwell Whyte was a real pioneer, having been led into this area twenty years earlier. In his little book *Dominion over Demons,* I read how he became involved.

In 1948 Maxwell Whyte had had a parishioner in his Toronto congregation who suffered from chronic asthma and was also a heavy smoker. For fourteen years the man had been a semi-invalid; prayers for healing seemed to avail nothing. One day another church member suggested to the pastor that the man's problem might be caused by a demon.

> We took the man into the church basement [Maxwell Whyte wrote] having read that demons sometimes came out crying with a loud voice, but of course we knew no one who had ever heard one come out! We had been taught to use the blood of Jesus in the presence of the destroyer, so we started to sing some choruses about the Blood. Then we attacked! "In the name of Jesus come out!"
>
> This was kept up, and as we pressed the battle hard the demons of asthma and smoking started to cough out, to vomit out. After one hour and twenty minutes we had seen a huge pile of handkerchiefs soaked with sputum, but he was healed! He stood up and breathed down to the bottom of his lungs and exclaimed, "Praise God, I am healed! I can breathe for the first time in my life!"
>
> The brother is still healed today, and no longer needs to smoke for Jesus set him free.

Maxwell Whyte began his lecture, Tuesday afternoon, with a discussion of deliverance in the New Testament, pointing out that Jesus had devoted almost a third of His public ministry to casting out demons. He also spoke of the danger of indulging in any form of psychic practice, stating that those who did so were disobeying the Scriptures and inviting attack by demon forces.

I was seated on the platform with him at the front of the auditorium when the first of a series of events occurred which were to dispel for good my doubts about the reality of evil spirits. A commotion in the audience drew everyone's eyes. Near the front of the room and to my left, a lanky, pimply-faced young man wearing thick glasses began moving restlessly on his chair, talking loudly to the embarrassed girl sitting beside him.

"He's lying, I tell you!" I heard him say. "Everything he says is a lie!" Suddenly he lunged to his feet and gave a shriek which electrified the audience. "He's lying . . . !"

Maxwell Whyte pointed a finger at him and said evenly, "Young

man, if you can control yourself, sit down and listen to the re-
mainder of the teaching. If you cannot, then go now to the prayer
room and we will minister to you later." I was greatly amazed to
see the incident had in no way shaken the lecturer's composure,
even though the audience, including me, was in a state of near
shock.

The youth was now trembling so violently that his glasses fell
from his face. Maxwell Whyte spoke quietly to some men sitting
nearby, who assisted the boy from the room. The girl who had
been sitting next to him scooped up his glasses and followed.

"What you have just witnessed," Maxwell Whyte addressed the
audience calmly once more, "is not unusual in a meeting where
the deliverance ministry is being introduced. The truth of deliverance often causes evil spirits to react in some such dramatic
manner. They seemed determined to interfere with this message
getting out."

I didn't hear too much of the rest of the talk. I was too stunned
by the turn of events. I was even more impressed with the authority and competence with which Maxwell Whyte had handled
the situation. Not one minister in a thousand would have remained
unruffled in the face of such an outburst, yet he had taken it in
stride. Obviously, he had faced such crises many times before.

A time for questions and ministry was scheduled for a small
room down the hall. About thirty people crowded into it. When
we had brought in enough chairs for everyone a small, pretty
brunette stood up.

"I consider myself a Christian," she began, "yet I feel I've been
greatly helped by some of the very practices you condemned in
your talk. I believe in extrasensory perception. I read my horo-
scope daily, and at times spirits from the other side have com-
municated with me, giving me helpful advice. I cannot accept the
authority of the Bible the way you do. It was written by men and
some of its teachings are cruel and judgmental. I have come to

believe in a God of total love and to reject the concept of hell and a devil."

"You are not alone," Maxwell Whyte answered gently. "Most of the modern world has come to believe that Satan and his angels do not exist. As a result, many Christians believe that everything supernatural must come from God. Nothing could be further from the truth."

The woman shook her head stubbornly. "But I tell you, my spirits are good and wise!"

Before Maxwell Whyte could answer, two men appeared at the door, propping between them the distraught young man who had been ushered out of the meeting. His girl friend followed.

"He's been asking for help, Reverend." They draped the youth into a chair, still trembling. Maxwell Whyte stood over the young man. "Spirit," his voice was suddenly stern, "I'm speaking to you and not to the man. In Jesus' name I command you to release this person and to come out!"

At these words, the young man erupted into a spasm of coughing quite similar to Joseph Wheeler's reaction when I had prayed for him at the altar in Florida. And when the coughing spell ended, he exhibited an almost identical relief. The shaking subsided, his facial expression returned to normal.

"I feel better." He smiled up at the girl. "I really do! In fact I feel great!"

As Maxwell Whyte counseled with the youth, I glanced over at the woman who had spoken moments before. She was obviously agitated, sitting on the edge of her seat making little moaning sounds, her fingers clenching and unclenching spasmodically. Suddenly her moans became an ear-splitting scream which bounced off the walls of the room, jangling anew the nerves of the thirty spectators not yet recovered from the auditorium antics of the young man. Two people jumped to their feet and rushed from the room. They had had enough.

Maxwell Whyte stepped to the woman's side. "Help me, Don," he called to me. My heart pounding, I came over and grasped one of the woman's wrists while he held the other. She sprang from the chair, twisting to break free of our grasp, her head flying back and forth so fast that her long brown hair stung my face like a whip. Then she opened her eyes. What gazed out at us was less than human.

Now from her lips came an eerie laugh, more sinister than anything I had ever heard. It sent shivers all the way down my spine. I didn't know what to do but hang onto her arm. I was shaken to my very depths.

"That laugh!" Maxwell Whyte exclaimed. "I'd recognize it anywhere. Witchcraft!"

At the mention of the word the woman let loose another screeching laugh. She was quite tiny, physically, slim and not more than five feet two inches tall. Nevertheless, she began to drag the two of us around the room as if we were small children. The people scattered before us like quail, pushing chairs out of our way, some cringing against the wall. I couldn't recall ever having been in so strange and terrifying a situation before.

At last, to my vast relief, Maxwell Whyte took dominion over the situation.

"You demon of witchcraft," his voice seemed to slice the very air with its authority. "You are subject to me in the name of Jesus Christ, and I command you to come out of this woman!"

Instantly the woman went limp in our grasp, giving a long protracted wail which finally dwindled away into silence. As we half-carried her to a chair, she began to weep softly. Maxwell Whyte caught my eye and smiled. "It's gone," he said. "It left with that long wail. I've seen the same thing dozens of times. The weeping is just relief."

Even as he spoke, the woman sat up. Fumbling in her skirt pocket she brought out a handkerchief and wiped her eyes. I was startled at the transformation in her face. Attractive before, now there was an added softness about her expression. Some harshness, some glare had dropped away.

"I'm sorry for the way I behaved just now," she said. "I couldn't seem to help myself." I knew what her face made me think of. A madonna. She looked around the room at the wondering faces. "Ever since I first became interested in psychic things, it has been as if some power has been drawing me to all kinds of strange meetings and compelling me to read strange books. I—I don't understand all that's happened here tonight, but I feel as if something terribly evil has gone away."

I don't recall a great deal about the next hour or so. There was more ministry, some questions and discussion, but I hardly heard, so occupied was I with the two events I had just witnessed. I felt I had learned enough to ponder for a month.

But before the week was out I was to take part in another scene which would affect me even more profoundly than the first. It was lunchtime the final day of the conference and the auditorium had begun to empty after the morning session when we heard sobbing in the back of the room. It was coming from a boy of maybe ten or eleven seated next to a white-haired lady. Maxwell Whyte and I both went back to them.

"Can you help my grandson?" The lady had one arm around the boy's shoulders protectively. Before we could ask what the trouble was, the child's body went rigid and his teeth began to chatter. Maxwell Whyte bent over him.

"You foul spirit, what are you?"

The boy's lips moved as the chattering continued. "Eh-eh-eh-eh . . ." At last he brought out the word which struck me like a physical blow.

"Epilepsy!"

Epilepsy? Epilepsy a spirit? As I stared, disbelieving, the small body began a spasmodic jerking. His grandmother nodded in confirmation. "We've taken him everywhere. We've tried everything."

The three of us lowered the unconscious boy to the floor. Then in the name of Jesus, Maxwell Whyte commanded the spirit of epilepsy to come out. Though the child seemingly remained unhearing, there was an instant reaction. He rolled on his side and began to cough, violently and repeatedly. A final convulsion shuddered his whole body and then he lay still. After about thirty seconds he opened his eyes and blinked up at the circle of faces.

"Do you—is he—he's never come out of a seizure this fast!" His grandmother's voice was quavery with hope.

"I hope he's through with them forever." Maxwell Whyte smiled at the boy, who was climbing slowly to his feet. "But sometimes there's a physical weakness or injury which allowed the spirit to enter in the first place." And putting his hands on the child's head, he prayed for a healing of body, mind, spirit.

"That's what's so bewildering about epilepsy," he said to me when the two had gone. "Sometimes it seems to be a purely physical, organic problem which this ministry is powerless to help. Other times it's quite clearly demon-based. I personally have known a number of sufferers from epilepsy to be instantly and permanently set free through a single deliverance ministry."

Alone in my room after lunch, I thought back over the events of the week. As amazing as it all had been, the incident which stirred me most was this little boy's deliverance. I took my Bible from my suitcase and thumbed through it until I found the passage I was looking for.

And when they came to the crowd, a man came up to him and kneeling before him said, "Lord, have mercy on my son, *for he is an epileptic* and he suffers terribly; for often he falls into the fire, and often into the water. And I brought him to your disciples, and they could not heal him." And Jesus answered, ". . . bring him here to me." And Jesus rebuked him, *and the demon came out of him,* and the boy was cured instantly. [Matthew 17:14–18 RSV]

A demon of epilepsy! Now I knew the reason our efforts in be-half of Irene Corbett had failed. Now I knew why her seizures had come so often during religious services. I knew what the evil, vicious thing was that had succeeded in taking her very life. In Irene, we had been battling not a mere disease or physical handicap; we had been battling a spiritual enemy. And we had battled without the one weapon we desperately needed, the deliverance ministry!

Returning home from Cleveland I realized that in the space of a few short days the Lord had removed every doubt from my mind. Demon spirits were real, and more important, deliverance from them in the name of Jesus Christ was real. I could no longer doubt, either, that in God's mysterious scheme of things I, personally, was being called to help reveal to His people the ministry He had provided to combat this particular form of satanic assault.

> And these signs shall follow them that believe; in my name shall they cast out devils . . . .

If I wondered what the next step was, I wasn't long in finding out. Much as I had learned in Cleveland, I was still a rank beginner in these areas. Now God seemed determined to expose me to an intensity of spiritual warfare which I would have been in no way ready for earlier.

Only a few evenings after I got back to Pompano Beach, Alice and I were at Jack and Anne Musselman's when there was a knock on the door.

"That will be Stella Sweeney," Anne said, getting up. The Musselmans had told us about Stella, and I was anxious to meet her. Stella had lived quite a life! A teen-age marriage had ended in divorce, leaving her with two sons to rear alone. By the time the boys were grown, Stella was a confirmed alcoholic, regularly partying it up in the New England town where she lived. Then a shattering automobile accident jarred her into Alcoholics Anonymous and sobriety. Later Stella moved to Florida where Christian friends led her to Jesus and prayed her through to the baptism in the Holy Spirit. The Musselmans told us she was now a radiant Christian, wonderfully changed in many ways. But she was still struggling against severe inner torments. All through the day "voices" taunted her and tempted her to return to the old wild life; at night there were recurring dreams.

Now Stella was standing just inside the door. A vivacious redhead, the shining eyes were those of a young and happy girl. She came in and joined our circle. For half an hour I talked about my experiences in Cleveland. I could tell that Stella was considering the accounts quite personally.

"I'm convinced I need deliverance too," she said finally. "I could feel something churning inside me even as you told those stories. Could we do it right here and now?"

I glanced at Jack and he nodded agreement.

"It's possible your problems don't have anything to do with evil spirits," I warned Stella. I asked what other approaches she had tried; perhaps it was just her "old self," her "carnal nature," that needed to be subjected to prayer, faithful seeking in the Bible, and obedience. But apparently she had followed these disciplines faithfully since her conversion, without the slightest effect on certain areas of her life.

We put Stella in a straight-backed chair in the middle of the room. I suggested that before we tried the deliverance she might want to pray, asking God's help in what we were going to do. Stella bowed her head, but for some reason she seemed to have difficulty speaking. She looked up in surprise.

"Something seems to be trying to choke me."

So instead, Alice voiced the prayer for her. Then with all of us gathered around Stella, I touched her lightly on the head and said, "In the name of Jesus Christ I take authority over any evil spirit tormenting this woman . . ." and that's as far as I got, for suddenly a harsh, sardonic laugh came from her throat. I glanced at her face. She was glaring up at me through eyes narrowed to hate-filled slits, her lips curled in a mocking sneer. It was like reliving a nightmare, like a re-enactment of the scene with the woman in Cleveland, only this time Maxwell Whyte wasn't on hand to take charge.

My heart began to hammer in my throat. I felt as if the evil thing staring at me out of Stella's eyes were measuring me in some way. Behind the sulphurous gaze I sensed a crafty intelligence. The lips parted.

"You're all a bunch of fools!"

My skin crawled. That was not Stella's voice. The smoldering eyes never left my face as it spoke again.

"This woman belongs to me."

I was dumb with shock, hypnotized by those eyes.

"This is my house. I live here and none of you can cast me out."

Wrenching my eyes from that gaze with an effort, I glanced at Alice, then at Jack and Anne. They were as stunned as I was. For a moment I felt an almost hysterical sense of relief that they were present. Nobody could believe what was happening unless they saw it with their own eyes!

Summoning all my courage I tried to speak with assurance and authority.

"Demon, I command you to give me your name."

Stella's face twisted even more grotesquely than before. "Hate!"

Involuntarily I jumped backward. I knew what I should do. I should command that spirit to come out. But before I could collect myself the voice came again, sly, dripping with sarcasm.

"She says she loves him."

"Loves who?" I asked the question automatically.

"You know who!" The voice was angry and petulant now. "Him . . . Jesus!"

The word was spat out like a curse. "But he can't have her,

she's mine! She's always been mine!" Once more that hideous laughter.

Suddenly I felt a tremendous indignation at the evil thing flaunting itself in Stella.

"You demon of hate," I said, "I charge you in the name of Jesus Christ to come out of this woman!"

To my astonishment both her arms shot straight up, the fingers of each hand curled like a claw, while a sound like the roar of a maddened animal came from her mouth. Just as suddenly she relaxed.

She pushed her hair out of her eyes with the back of one hand and smiled shakily. Her blue eyes were clear once more.

"Thank you, Jesus! Thank you, Jesus!" she said. Then to my surprise she pressed her hands sharply to her sides.

"There are more! I can hear them arguing inside me!"

Although I knew the Bible spoke of more than one evil spirit inhabiting a person, I had never considered it a current possibility. Stella closed her eyes and we watched in amazement as her face changed into the caricature of a pouting child. If I hadn't known better I would have sworn Stella was putting on an act.

"In the name of Jesus," I addressed myself to the thing manifesting itself, "I command you to tell me who you are."

Stella cocked her head and from her mouth came a high, whiny voice—quite different from either Stella's natural voice or the metallic tone of the demon of hate.

"We don't like her new friends," the voice complained. "She's no fun anymore. And we miss the music!" By now Stella's whole body was swaying rhythmically on the chair. She began humming tunelessly and snapping her fingers as if in time to music we couldn't hear.

"That's enough!" I cried. "I command you in the name of Jesus to name yourself!"

The answer came in a shrill voice, "Vanity!"

On command, the second spirit left with a whine. For two unbelievable hours we continued ministering to this woman, the strangest experience of my life up to that moment, even more incredible than the happenings in Cleveland. Twenty-two different spirits came out, each one arguing and complaining before it left. If Stella had been the greatest character actress of the century and if she had rehearsed her role for a year, she could not have played half so many parts half so convincingly. Some of the distorted expressions her face assumed, some of the exaggerated voices, had to be seen and heard to be believed.

When the twenty-second spirit was cast out, Stella wept with the sheer joy of freedom. After she had gone, Alice and I remained with Jack and Anne, talking about what we had seen until the early hours of the morning.

In the weeks that followed I found myself talking about deliverance nearly everywhere I spoke. And every time I brought the subject up, no matter how briefly, I ended up casting out demons afterward. But even as I gained a certain measure of experience there were troublesome questions. Questions I couldn't answer.

One night in Pennsylvania, after I had ministered deliverance, an elderly man spoke to me. "Reverend Basham, I came to the prayer room because I thought I needed deliverance, but nothing happened when you prayed over me. Now I'm confused. Do I have a demon or not? How can I tell?"

As so often before, it was a question I didn't have an answer for.

Back home in Pompano Beach I got out the notebook I had started what seemed now a long time ago. At the top of a fresh page I wrote: *How can we know if we have a demon?* Then I leaned back and sifted an accumulation of experiences. The more I considered them the more I came to feel that the key lay in the area of our "hang-ups." From years of counseling I knew that people's recurring, chronic personal problems tended to fall into one of three categories. They would tell me:

I have trouble with sex. My mind will not leave it alone. In certain areas the slightest suggestivity captures my sexual instincts and I am off, lured into a mire of fantasy and desire. I have no control over these thoughts. They bully me, enslave me. My willpower is to no avail; prayer is empty.

I am ridden by a certain emotion. Anger, worry, fear, frustration, resentment, jealousy. I cannot praise, I cannot be thankful. This emotion has not yielded to counseling or prayer. It keeps me from a closer walk with God.

I am hooked on some addicting agent. Society itself is part of the problem. Tobacco is thrust at me in every ad. Alcohol is held up as a social necessity. Pills to wake me up, put me to sleep, take away my pain, tranquilize me, expand my mind. I am a slave to a drug.

The baffling thing was that all of these hang-ups were—at certain times and with certain people—subject to prayer, self-control, relinquishment. My own battle with money, for example. Once I had taken the great leap of faith and moved into a new dependence on the Lord, money worries largely disappeared. That was real victory. Other times the same effort, devotion, commitment produced no change at all. Could it be that this was one of the principal criteria for demon affliction? I drew up a sample test.

A Test for an Evil Spirit

1. Treat your hang-up first as a simple carnal sin and see what happens. Confess it, ask forgiveness, believe that forgiveness has been granted. Now apply will, discipline, and prayer to the habit patterns that have entrenched themselves in this area. Whenever they reappear, put them "under the crucifixion" of Jesus, knowing that He is able when we are not.
2. If all of this produces no victory, you may be dealing with a demon—and you should seek deliverance.

As I wrote, I was remembering an interview I had had following a church service in Miami. The woman and I sat down in a front pew after the church had emptied. She seemed calm enough until

I asked her why she felt she needed help. Her voice immediately grew sharp.

"Don't talk to me like that!" she snapped. "You're trying to make me out to be an adulteress!" Even as she spoke the words, she realized nothing had been said about adultery. She lowered her head and began to weep. "I don't know what made me say such a thing."

"Have you ever had such an experience?"

"No."

"But you have thoughts about it?"

"That's the trouble. I can't get them out of my head. They come in and harangue and harass me and push me around. It's just by the grace of God that I haven't . . . that I haven't . . . I've even been to a psychiatrist. He helped me understand a lot of things—but I still have the thoughts."

There was the pattern. A person pushed around in some area of his life. Serious efforts made to change, to no avail. In that instance, responding to what I had said about deliverance in my sermon, the woman had asked if there could be such a thing as a spirit of adultery. When I said it was possible, she had prayed, confessing her problem and renouncing any spirit that might be involved. When I commanded it to come out, she had experienced a definite sense of "lightness." Two months later a letter came: she had been "gloriously free" from the unwelcome thoughts ever since.

It wasn't long afterward that I discovered another indication that a demon might be at work. One evening Alice and I were having dinner with a group of friends in West Palm Beach. Over coffee the conversation came around—as it usually did by now—to the subject of deliverance. Right in the middle of the story about the woman in Cleveland with the spirit of witchcraft, one of the guests, Bertha Matthews, suddenly banged her fist on the table, rattling the dishes and startling all of us.

"That's the biggest bunch of nonsense I ever heard!" she exclaimed. "I don't believe a word of it. Besides, it's a perfectly loathsome subject to bring up at the dinner table!" Bertha was trembling and her eyes began to fill with tears. She jumped up from the table and rushed from the room. Her husband, his face red with embarrassment, murmured an apology about his wife "having trouble with her nerves lately."

"Basham, you've done it again!" I silently berated myself. Aloud I said, "I had no idea the story would upset anyone. Please forgive me for causing such a scene."

"It's not your fault," Mr. Matthews tried to reassure me. "Bertha *has* been nervous lately."

In the living room Bertha rejoined us. "I want to apologize to everyone for flying off the handle," she said. Her voice was still shaky. "I don't know what's the matter with me. I wonder, Don, if you would pray for me."

Bertha sat down and watched—I thought—a little apprehensively as I crossed the room to her. Supposing that I should use the same techniques I had used before, I laid one hand gently on her head and began, "In the name of Jesus I come against any evil spirit in this—"

With a startled cry she knocked my hand away and jumped to her feet. "No, no!" she almost shouted. "I don't want you casting anything out of me! I just wanted you to say a prayer." She was backing out of the room, still eyeing me with caution. The look on her face reminded me suddenly of Mrs. Stern in Sharon years before.

It seemed to me that the evening was ruined. I had spoiled a dinner party. How often in this ministry I was involved in little tension-filled situations like this. When we left a few minutes later, I felt like an outcast.

The next morning, however, I had a telephone call from one of the women who had been there. "I thought you'd like to know what happened last night!" Her voice was enthusiastic. "After you and Alice left, Bertha and her husband changed their minds about Bertha's needing deliverance. They asked *me* to pray with them. Frankly, I was scared stiff, but I agreed anyhow. I just prayed for help and guidance and then I commanded any evil spirit to come out of her. I hadn't even *finished* when Bertha gave a kind of little cough and started crying—crying for joy. You just wouldn't *believe* the change in her! She looked absolutely radiant. What do you make of it? Do you think it really was a deliverance?"

I did think so! I could see tremendous possibilities for the future right at that moment. The possibility of a whole Church enabled to claim Jesus' promise that when the Son sets us free we are free indeed!

I went back to my notes. Under the heading "How Can We Know if We Have a Demon?" I wrote:

A. The modern term "hang-up" *may* be descriptive of demonic activity. Are we *stuck* at a point in our spiritual development? Is the problem subject to prayer and obedience? If not, we should at least consider demons as a cause.

B. If ever we feel *compelled* to destructive acts, it may be that an evil spirit is at work.

C. An especially strong negative reaction to the idea of deliverance should raise the question, where does this reaction come from? Certainly there are realistic objections to this ministry; are these objections based on realism, or are they coming from another source—perhaps the demons themselves?

I turned the page and wrote across the top another heading, another question that had long haunted and perplexed me. I did not realize as I put down the words what unpleasant memories they would shortly unlock. The question I set myself to explore was: "How Do Demons Get Inside Us in the First Place?"

10

How They Get In

WHERE'S Laura?"

"I don't know, Mother," Lisa said. "She was with me across the street a little while ago."

"Lisa, how many times have I told you two girls to stay together?" Alice's voice was disapproving. "Now you go find her. It's almost time for dinner!"

"All right, Mother," Lisa sighed like a martyr. "I'll go find her."

But Lisa couldn't find Laura, and neither could Shari or Glenn. Alice and I joined the search, Alice going one way and I another.

"The children down the street said they thought she was in the park," Alice said as we met again in front of the house. "But when I walked over there the park was empty."

"I'll drive around the block. She can't be far away." I tried to sound less concerned than I felt. But the drive around the neighborhood also proved fruitless. Alice was standing by the driveway when I turned in. Her face fell when she saw me get out of the car alone.

"The others haven't seen a sign of her either," Alice's voice was beginning to sound shaky. "Think we should call the police? It will be dark soon."

"I don't know," I shrugged, still not wanting to admit my fear.

And at that moment, walking down the sidewalk as if nothing were wrong, came the familiar little figure of our Laura. Alice gave a glad cry and rushed toward her. Then she stopped, anger rising through her relief.

"Laura Anne Basham, where have you been! Didn't you hear us call you? Don't you know we've been looking for you everywhere?"

Laura's blue eyes were innocent. "I was over at Gina's."

"Then you should have heard us calling!"

"We were playing in the garage." Laura still sounded unconcerned.

"But we thought you were lost, Laura! Don't you understand?" Tears of exasperation were starting to course down Alice's cheeks. "We thought you were lost, Laura," she repeated. *"We thought we would never see our Laura Anne again!"*

At last Laura understood. Burying her face in Alice's skirt, she begain to wail in terror. Alice and I looked at each other. After all she hadn't really been lost, just playing in a neighbor's garage.

"It's all right, Laura," I patted her on the head. "We're not angry any more. You just frightened us, that's all. We love you and don't want anything to happen to you."

But Laura was unconsolable. She clung to her mother like a burr and gasped between sobs, "I . . . I didn't m-mean to be bad! I'm—I'm sorry!"

"Daddy said it's all right now, Laura," Alice bent over and hugged the trembling little form. "We're all back together now and it's all right."

Laura raised her tear-stained face. "But you said I might never see you again!" And she burst into renewed wailing. Alice looked at me helplessly.

"What do we do now? First we couldn't make her understand and now we can't get her calmed down."

Laura sniffled her way through most of the dinner hour, and it wasn't until we all piled into the car to drive downtown for ice cream afterward that she finally seemed pacified.

By the children's bedtime I had forgotten the incident. But when I went in to say goodnight, I found Laura sitting bolt upright in her bed. I reached over to turn off the light.

"Lie down now, honey," I said.

Laura's lower lip began to quiver. "I can't sleep, Daddy."

"Why not?"

" 'Cause every time I start to say my prayers, *something inside of me makes fun of them.*" And she began to cry.

Leaving the light on I sat down on the bed and for a few moments pondered her strange statement. Something inside of her? I couldn't recall ever having heard any of our children say such a thing before. Reluctant as I was to think it, it sounded precisely like the activity of some demonic, mocking spirit. What a frightening idea, that such a thing could invade my own child!

I tried to sound casual as I made the suggestion to Laura. "You know, honey, that sounds a little like it might be an evil spirit."

"Uh-huh."

"Want to get rid of it?"

Laura nodded. I was grateful that the children knew about the ministry I was getting into and accepted it quite naturally.

"Let's ask Jesus to help us, okay?" I said

Laura nodded again and said a simple little prayer asking Jesus to chase away the teasing thing inside her. When she finished I said, "Let's find out the spirit's name, then I'll tell it to leave."

"All right, Daddy."

From what Laura had said I had assumed the spirit's name

would be mockery, but to my surprise, when I commanded it to name itself, Laura answered firmly, "Fear." As I ordered the spirit of fear to come out, Laura grabbed herself across the midriff. Then she straightened up.

"I felt it leave," she said matter-of-factly. "I'm fine now. G'nite, Daddy." And she snuggled down against her pillow.

"Goodnight, sweetheart." I stood up relieved and still very puzzled.

"Daddy?" Laura's sleepy voice reached me at the door. "I think I know when that old spirit came in."

"You do? When?"

"Well, you know this afternoon when you and Mommy were so mad at me? And you said you might never ever see me again? Daddy, I got *so scared!* And I've felt something laughing, ever since."

Guilt swept over me as I recalled how Alice and I, determined to make a point with Laura, had succeeded only in terrifying her. Was it possible that on that terror an alien spirit of fear had come riding in?

This was how I began to explore, quite by accident within my own family, the ways in which an evil spirit can gain entry into the system. What happened with Laura, I felt, was that because of the afternoon's trauma a crack appeared in her natural defenses. As a child of God she was ordinarily protected from such invasions. Actually, however, it must work out often for us that because of some disturbance—a shock, an illness, an accident— our normal defenses are let down. Obviously, it doesn't take long for an evil spirit to take advantage of the situation, get in, and start doing his dirty work.

It wasn't long before I began to run across other Ports of Entry. One day in McKeesport, Pennsylvania, a lovely teen-age girl came forward after a church service where I had spoken on deliverance.

"Is there a lady here who could pray for me? It's about demons."

"A lady?"

"Yes, it's very personal."

It happened that one of the deconesses of the McKeesport church had had some experience in deliverance. She and the girl disappeared into a prayer room. It wasn't until later that I discovered the reason for this beautiful teen-ager's bashfulness. She had been plagued by a compulsive desire to throw herself sexually at men. Sure enough, the demon within her named itself "wantonness."

"But the interesting thing to me," the deaconess continued, "was how the spirit got into Maria in the first place. She identified very clearly the time the spirit entered: 'I know' she told me, 'that I invited these feelings inside of me when I started going to those sex movies.' "

Beneath the heading, "How Do Demons Get Inside?" I jotted down in my notebook two tentative answers.

Spirits invade us through chinks in our natural armor caused by trauma.

Spirits take hold of our natural carnal desires when they are indulged to excess.

In Maria's case it was deliberate exposure to the hyperstimulation of certain films. For another person it might be overindulging a natural appetite for food or drink. Any repeated indulgence of "the flesh" could provide the point of low resistance where a spirit could enter in. Our appetites are areas to which we can say yes or no. If we habitually say yes, we open ourselves to the possibility of something other than mere appetite taking root within us.

I must confess my reluctance to admit the seriousness of a third Port of Entry. My first inkling of it had come during

Maxwell Whyte's warning at Cleveland about the dangers of dabbling in occultism. The bloodcurdling scene in the smaller room as we wrestled with the demon of witchcraft was scarred in my memory. But I told myself it was a special case, an exception. The fact was, I didn't want to grant that all psychic excursions carried a danger. Hadn't Alice and I, years ago, been quite deeply involved in this whole area? And though we had decided, after a while, that we wanted no part of it, what harm had it actually done?

And then I had two experiences in close succession which tended to confirm everything Maxwell Whyte had said and to make me look again at what Alice and I had been through. One day in northern Florida a woman came to the prayer meeting where I was speaking. As was usually the case now, I included in my talk Christ's promise of freedom from bondage through the deliverance ministry. As I was speaking I noticed this particular woman sitting forward on the edge of her seat, her eyes fixed on me with a strange glare. Even after the meeting had been dismissed she remained motionless in her seat, her eyes riveted on me. As I stepped toward her she shrank back against her chair and began to whimper.

"They say I'll die!"

On command the spirit tormenting her spoke its name:

"Fortune-telling."

I was surprised, but helped her to a successful deliverance. In the next few minutes several other spirits were identified and cast out, among them necromancy and palm-reading. Afterward the woman confessed that she had often consulted fortune-tellers.

"It was a hobby of mine," she admitted, "until about three years ago when a palm-reader told me that I would not live beyond the age of fifty. I'm fifty-two now, and the last two years have been a nightmare. Every time I become even slightly ill, I'm sure I'm dying."

And I had always dismissed fortune-telling as a harmless parlor game!

Very shortly thereafter I was ministering to a man who suffered from periods of deep suicidal depression. At one point he said rather casually, "You know I visited a medium after my wife died. I was looking for some evidence that she was still alive." A number of strange, unexplainable things had happened at the medium's home. Messages purporting to be from his wife were passed on, some of them containing information known only to the two of them. But always, after the séances, he was tormented with thoughts of taking his own life.

I was more bewildered than ever. Could it be that simply by visiting a medium or having your fortune told you were exposing yourself to demonic oppression? What exactly was the relationship between psychic experience and Satan's realm?

Once more I lined up my notebook, my Bible, and a concordance, and began to check the scriptural references to occult practice. I was dismayed and astounded at what my research revealed—not only at the overwhelming amount of Scripture which forbade such practices, but also at the severity of God's judgment against those who pursued them. From the Bible, one thing became crystal clear; *God considers all occult practices abominable and idolatrous.* Over forty references in both Old and New Testaments confirmed it. According to Scripture it is as sinful for a child of God to seek supernatural help in the occult realm as it is for him to commit adultery.

> And the soul that turneth after such as have familiar spirits, and after wizards . . . I will even set my face against that soul, and will cut him off from among his people. [Leviticus 20:6]

> Now the works of the flesh are manifest, which are these: adultery, fornication, uncleanness, lasciviousness, idolatry, witchcraft . . . of the which I tell you . . . that they which do such things shall not inherit the Kingdom of God. [Galatians 5:19–21]

It was all beginning to make sense. It would be so completely typical of Satan to produce a lie-world of the supernatural, a whole realm of counterfeit spiritual experience. Oh, real enough in the sense of being authentically supernatural! But a deadly counterfeit in that it places the innocent seeker, not in touch with God, or the spirits of departed loved ones, as he supposes, but with the very powers of darkness themselves.

The difficulty of course is that it *does,* at first, seem innocent. Alice and I had had no sense of disobedience when we set out to investigate psychic phenomena.

It was my first year of seminary. Because we had heard fascinating stories about it, Alice and I started attending a Spiritualist church which met on Sunday nights in a home on the edge of town. The leader was a trance-medium, one who after entering into a state of self-induced sleep becomes the medium through which a purported spirit from the other side can communicate. In this case the spirit claimed to be that of the medium's dead sister.

The Sunday night rituals were much the same each week. From ten to fifteen persons gathered in the medium's home and before the service each of us would write out a question on a small slip of paper and place it in a basket on the table behind which sat the medium. During the singing of an old-fashioned gospel hymn the medium would tie a blindfold across her eyes, then rest her head on her arms and enter into a state of trance. As soon as the music stopped she would sit up and the voice claiming to be her sister would speak through her lips.

"Good evening friends, this is Minnie Marie Blackburn speaking to you from the world of spirit." We never questioned the hackneyed greeting which sounded more like an announcer on amateur radio than a spirit presumably descended from realms of light. After some small talk, "Minnie" would begin to answer the questions in the basket. She did this without touching the basket or the papers containing the question. The meetings were all conducted in the open, in bright light, where the proceedings could be viewed clearly.

For example, "Minnie" would say: "This question is from my sister's earthly neighbor who asks if she should sell her property for the price offered. Her spirit guide says that she should not be in a hurry to sell. The property is worth more than she has been offered."

And indeed, such a question was among those in the basket.

Alice and I were utterly intrigued. "Minnie" on occasion would give descriptions of what it was like on the other side: "Beautiful gardens are here, palatial homes, teachers happily welcoming new arrivals from the earth plane. Everyone is happy here, everyone helping everyone else." Fascinated, I didn't notice "Minnie's" total omission of the name of Jesus Christ. She called what she was doing "preaching the gospel of God."

Alice and I attended the strange services for a considerable period. Then one Sunday night there was a startling disclosure. Speaking through "Minnie," a spirit who claimed he was Dr. Samuel Johnson, the famous eighteenth-century English writer, declared that he was searching for a "clear channel" through whom he could communicate to the modern world. To my astonishment I was to be that instrument. While he was pleased with my desire to go into the ministry, "Dr. Johnson" made it clear that I would be a much more effective channel for good by becoming a medium.

Now it was what happened next which convinced me that we were truly dealing with the supernatural. For as proof of his having watched me closely for a long period of time, "Dr. Johnson" revealed certain things to the group which I had done in the past about which no one knew except myself. He spoke for example of a time I had been praying in the Spirit while driving a car across the plains of Oklahoma. He also predicted the surprise return of my brother Fred from Greenland—a prediction which shortly came true. "Dr. Johnson" concluded by urging me to set aside a period each day for contemplation so that he could begin to speak to me directly.

Amazing! Truly amazing! Why then did it also make me feel vaguely uneasy?

Just a slight wariness at first. Just a feeling that this might not be the will of God, without knowing why I felt that way. It would be dishonest to say that this feeling came quickly. My desire for continued supernatural experience was very strong. Only some inner alarm kept sounding inside me. To complicate matters, in my classes at the seminary the authority of Scripture was much in question. Therefore, I found myself tending to discount the one or two warnings I was aware of in the Bible against spiritualism. After all, what I was experiencing was far more exciting than dull Bible reading.

So I ignored the warnings at first. And then some rather strange things started to happen to me. Several times, when I was praying or reading alone, I seemed to be aware of some invisible person in the room with me. I sensed very clearly that I was being watched. On one occasion I thought I saw the faint but discernible outline of a human figure standing nearby. When I stared straight at it, it disappeared. But each time I went back to reading, I would see it once more out of the corner of my eye.

And once, when I was browsing in the campus bookstore, I felt an irresistible urge to tilt my head upward. My attention was suddenly riveted on a book on the very top shelf. The book was in the middle of a long line of reference volumes and there was no earthly reason for my seeing it. My heart jumped, for it was the biography of Dr. Samuel Johnson.

The following Sunday night I reported to "Minnie" the strange happenings of the week past. I received a most enthusiastic endorsement. I was strongly encouraged to continue the same kind of openness to the spirit world.

"Don, are you sure this is right?" Alice's words as we drove home that evening echoed my own question. And soon it was stronger than a question: a voice insistently repeating, "Stay away. Stay away." The idea of giving over my personality to the control of another—no matter how eminent—frightened me. I asked God to show Alice and me if we were getting involved in something that was dangerous.

The next Sunday night during the trance I told the spirit control that I was not convinced it was God's will for me to go on in this area. "Minnie" was clearly disappointed. Later on I noticed the medium, still in trance, began to twist and writhe on the chair. Suddenly "Minnie" said that she was relinquishing control of her sister because of "spiritual interference" but that she would try to get back in touch with her in half an hour. Then the medium slumped forward and came out of the trance gasping for breath.

She was quite obviously frightened, but within half an hour she agreed to submit to the trance again. She replaced her blindfold and within seconds "Minnie" was once more in control. But this time it was different. The spirit voice was now aggrieved and complaining, the medium clearly experiencing discomfort.

"Minnie's" last words made chills run up my spine. "The interruption was caused by the intrusion of an unwelcome spirit," the voice lamented. "This spirit controlled—during his earth life— our father. He hated me and my sister. A few minutes ago he forced his way into our circle . . . ." The voice became shrill and tremulous. "He attempted to take my sister's life by inserting his fingers into her windpipe." With that the medium collapsed with her head in her arms, and the trance ended.

So did our visits to the medium's home!

Although I understood nothing of the motive or means of the

attack, that attempted "murder from heaven" convinced me that our prayer had been answered. We were in an area God did not want us to have anything to do with. We never went back.

My sense of disillusionment was keen. The fascination of Spiritualism had had a strong grip on me. Like many another Christian I had been eager for demonstrable spiritual reality. But recognizing that God had shut the door, I determined never to attend another Spiritualist séance.

Looking back on this bizarre period from the vantage point of my present involvement in the deliverance ministry I realized that Alice and I had become involved in a satanic deception. We were, in that medium's living room, in contact with spirits all right—demon spirits who were only impersonating the spirits of deceased human beings. I also saw significance in the fact that the writhing and choking which the medium endured during that attack was the same kind of physical manifestation I had seen in many people who were being delivered. It was as though Satan's henchmen, when threatened (perhaps by my expression of doubt?), had revealed their true nature—beings out only to hurt and destroy.

Apparently then, evil spirits could gain a foothold in human life by our participation in forbidden psychic practices as well as by our deliberate indulgence of physical appetites, and by various accidents, shocks, or traumatic experiences which "fractured" the personality and made it vulnerable.

How could we defend ourselves against such invasions? I wrote the following:

To Protect Ourselves

1. Do not deliberately indulge inappropriate carnal appetites.
2. Practice "pleading the blood." This is an ancient form of asking for divine protection; it entails claiming our rights as Christians to be protected from the evil one. Jesus defeated

Satan by going to the Cross and shedding His blood. We can claim that victory for ourselves. ("And they overcame him [Satan] by the blood of the Lamb, and the word of their testimony." Revelation 12:11.) Such a "pleading" seems especially helpful in times of traumatic experience such as an injury, a shock, a nightmare dream, a serious illness, or the like.

3. Stay strictly away from the psychic, medium, astrological, fortune-telling, ESP, Spiritualist world. If we have already come into contact with this world, confess such involvement as a sin, and seek deliverance.

As soon as I had written these last words I knew that I must do this myself.

I chose a time when I was alone in the house. First of all, as I had said in my notes, I confessed my involvement with Spiritualism as a sin. I laid the whole series of events before God as honestly as I could, admitting the great attraction I had felt for supernatural "special knowledge" and how I had ignored the warnings in His word. I asked Him to forgive me.

And then I prayed for deliverance. I wasn't sure it was possible to do this without the help of another, but I did not want to wait.

I spoke out loud: "In the name of Jesus Christ, I come against any occult spirit that may have entered me. I renounce you in the name of Jesus Christ and I command you—" And that was as far as I got.

A sudden wave of nausea swept over me. For a few seconds I had the strangest feeling that I didn't really want to renounce the spirit, that it was wrong to pray this way, that I needed and desperately wanted to continue my psychic investigation. I felt the same intense attraction that had goaded me into it years ago. I had to force myself to complete the command.

"In the name of Jesus, I command you, you demon of Spiritualism, to come out!"

Immediately my chest constricted and I exploded into a sharp spasm of coughing lasting perhaps seven or eight seconds. It left me red-faced, shaky, and astonished. Although I had by that time seen or assisted at several hundred exorcisms, I had not until that moment experienced anything myself whatsoever. What had happened?

Certainly, during the days that followed I noticed a distinct difference in my attitude toward everything psychic. Before, I had tended to regard such things as horoscopes and Ouija boards with a kind of benign toleration. Now my inner reaction was one of acute loathing and disgust. And as I continued to pray and thank God, I came to know without question that something had left me which had lodged inside me for a long, long time.

Had I known how to continue the self-deliverance, far more drastic results might have been forthcoming.

11

What We're Up Against

DO YOU know that I could actually *feel* something happening?" I said to Alice as I described my experience with the occult spirit.

I was sitting at my kitchen-alcove desk while she peeled potatoes at the sink. "Kind of a nausea—as though I were going to be sick." Having the thing actually happen to me had made a deeper impression than any amount of simple observing. Because many deliverances occurred without any physical symptoms at all, I had tended to believe that such things were not important. Now I drew up a list of all the different physical manifestations I had seen, noting again how ugly most of them were. I recalled Mark 1:26: "And the unclean spirit, convulsing him, and crying with a loud voice, came out of him." Yes, I'd seen that very reaction. "Listen to this list, Alice," I said.

> screams
> shaking
> convulsions
> weeping

> hysterical laughter
> writhing
> fainting
> sighing
> groaning
> choking
> gagging
> retching
> actual vomiting

Alice laid down her paring knife. "Do you mind, Don?" she said. "While I'm fixing supper?"

I closed my notebook with apologies. And yet I had the feeling that the very loathsomeness of some of these manifestations was trying to tell me something, something I had not yet grasped. As I wandered into the living room my mind went to a tape recording a friend had sent me some weeks back. It seemed to me there was more on that tape, too, than I had heard on a first listening. I got out our machine and put it on.

The tape contained the testimony of a minister who specialized in the field of pastoral counseling. During his training the Reverend David Lawson became proficient in the use of hypnosis * as an aid in counseling emotionally disturbed people. The strange results of one such counseling venture were most relevant to my own investigation. David's voice came from the recorder:

> I was put in touch with a young woman in her twenties, Judy, and had been counseling with her for several weeks. Judy was a Christian girl, with deep religious convictions, but with severe emotional problems which she seemed incapable of facing. So I resorted to putting her under hypnosis that I might speak to her inner consciousness, which I called the "Inner Judy."
> One day when I was talking to Inner Judy something startling happened. Another voice—a harsh voice quite unlike Judy's— spoke out through her lips. It said, "I don't want her to live be-

---

* Hypnosis itself can lead to demonic activity.

cause she wants to serve the Lord. I am not Judy. I want to kill Judy."

I didn't know what to make of it. But I was fascinated and wanted to learn more. So a few days later when Judy was once more under hypnosis I said to her, "Inner Judy I want to speak to that other voice." Immediately the same harsh voice I had heard before responded.

"What do you want?" it said.

I said, "What is your name? Who are you?"

The voice answered rather slyly, "Well, we have a lot of names. Some call us Satan, some call us demons."

Of course I couldn't accept that. "Now come on, Judy, you don't expect me—" The voice interrupted me.

"My name is *not* Judy! Don't call me by that name! You don't believe I'm from Satan, do you?"

"I certainly do not!" I replied emphatically.

"All right then, I'll prove it to you," the voice boasted. And then it proceeded to tell me intimate details of my private life which no other human being could possibly know.

I was absolutely stunned. "Let me speak to Inner Judy again," I said. "Inner Judy, do you know there's some kind of strange, uncanny power inside you?"

"Yes I know that," Inner Judy said sadly.

"Does Outer Judy know it?"

"No. The demons—there are a lot of them—said they would kill me if I told my conscious self they were inside."

In the weeks that followed, the foreign voice became more and more threatening. Sometimes during the counseling sessions the demons seemingly took over, suppressing Judy's own personality entirely.

It frightened David Lawson. The spirits boasted that they would not let her go and that it was their intent to kill her. One evening they tried to throw her out the window. David had to grab her. He was a large man, over six feet tall, weighing 210 pounds, while Judy weighed scarcely half that. But it took all of David's strength to restrain her. When finally the demons released their control, and he brought Judy out of her hypnosis, she looked at him pleadingly and said, "Help me before it's too late."

David tried calling his minister and his psychiatrist friends—none had any advice. Then, suddenly, he remembered an old preacher uncle of his—a minister in some small Pentecostal denomination—whom he had not seen in several years. He remembered the old man talking often about demons and demon possession. He also remembered his own reaction at the time—it was all nonsense. Pentecostal fanaticism.

But now I was desperate for help [the tape continued] and since my uncle lived not too far away I called him on the telephone and told him about Judy.

"What makes you think she's demon-possessed?" my uncle asked.

"Because, Uncle Charlie, she told me things about myself she had no way of knowing," I replied.

"That would be typical of demons," my uncle agreed. "They become so arrogant and boastful they just can't resist the temptation to reveal themselves." My uncle said he would minister to Judy.

The deliverance took several different sessions to complete. A real battle transpired in which there was much gagging and choking as demon after demon left her. But in the end the young woman was completely delivered. Today she is happily married, living a victorious Christian life free from the goading spirits which tormented her for so many years.

I turned off the recorder, opened my notebook again, and made the following observations about evil spirits as they were demonstrated in the Judy tape.

What We Are Up Against in the Deliverance Ministry

1. Demons act like their master, Satan.
2. Demons are physically strong.
3. Demons have pride-filled natures.
4. Many demons can live in a person at the same time.
5. Demons are filthy.
6. Demons are not to be feared in Christ.

Over the next few days I filled in further details under each of the six headings, drawing both from the Judy tape and from other experiences.

1. DEMONS ACT LIKE THEIR MASTER, SATAN

Satan's role among us, according to Scripture, is to steal, kill and destroy (John 10:10). We can expect his agents to do exactly the same.

Demons will try to steal. They seek our peace of mind, our assurance, our health.

In New England I once ministered to a fearful woman who was suffering nightly heart palpitations. Her husband had died of a heart attack some years before and she was convinced she would die in the same manner.

She was delivered from a spirit identified as "fear of heart failure" and the same night went to sleep without a pounding heart for the first time in five years. She still writes me regularly; her deliverance stands. The devil was out to steal her sleep and her enjoyment of life as well as her health.

Demons will try to kill. Demons had hurled Irene Corbett down a flight of stairs; they tried to throw Judy out a window. While I was attending a charismatic seminar in Minnesota a Lutheran pastor took me to visit a parishioner, a young mother who was suffering frequent acute respiratory seizures. She would wake up in the middle of the night straining and gasping for air, and even in the middle of the day would often become panic-stricken for lack of breath. On several occasions she had been hospitalized, although doctors could find no medical reason for her condition.

When we ministered to her, a spirit which identified itself as a "choking demon" was dislodged from her throat. Before it left, however, it blurted out this information: "When she was three years old, her mother was feeding her a spoonful of peanut butter and she began to choke. That's when I came in! I was waiting for my chance! I wanted to choke her! I wanted to kill her!"

Demons will try to destroy. I was standing in the back of a small church in Miami where I had been the Sunday evening speaker when a heavy-set woman with a tormented face came up and introduced herself. She told me she had been troubled for years by an uncontrollable temper.

"It terrifies me, Reverend Basham! You were talking about demons and how violent they can be? I get so violent I start screaming. I smash things—even things I care about. I'm actually frightened for my children. So far, I've never hurt a person, but who knows? One of these days I may . . . I might even . . . can you help me?"

The demon we cast out that night identified itself as "destruction." I still see this lady occasionally: she has not been plagued by the compulsion to break things since that time.

2. DEMONS ARE PHYSICALLY STRONG

Judy's hypernatural strength when the demons were in control was an example of this. I myself had experienced the same uncanny physical force in Cleveland. This attribute of demons is commented on in the Bible: ". . . and no one could bind him anymore, even with a chain; for he had often been bound with fetters and chains, but the chains he wrenched apart, and the fetters he broke in pieces; and no one had the strength to subdue him." [Mark 5:3 RSV]

Again in the account in Acts 19, seven men attempt to minister deliverance to a single afflicted individual. "And the man in whom the evil spirit was leaped on them, mastered all of them, and overpowered them, so that they fled out of that house naked and wounded."

I ran across similar descriptions in contemporary writing. In *Ever-Increasing Faith,* a collection of sermons by the famous evangelist Smith-Wigglesworth, is this story:

> I received a telegram once urging me to visit a case about two hundred miles from my home. As I went to this place I met the father and mother and found them broken-hearted. They led me up a staircase to a room where I saw a young woman on the floor and five people were holding her down. She was a frail young woman but the power in her was greater than all those young men.

3. DEMONS HAVE PRIDE-FILLED NATURES

They are proud of their accomplishments and often insist, as in the Judy tape, on their due recognition. One night at Jack and Anne Musselman's when we got into deliverance, I noticed Debbie, a teen-age friend of our daughter, Cindi, crouched in a corner, eyes wide with terror. Alice and I ministered to her and almost immediately a demon of fear left.

With Debbie looking calm and composed once more, Alice and I returned to our seats.

"Wait a minute!" Debbie's voice was sharp.

I turned to find her looking at me strangely. Then she laughed a mean little laugh and raised both hands, fingers spread wide apart.

"See these?"

The nails were bitten so far into the quick the end of each finger resembled an angry red bulb.

"That's what I do to her!" the voice speaking out of Debbie taunted. "She'll never have pretty hands as long as I'm here!"

Then the voice grew boastful. "You can't make me leave. She'll always bite her nails! Nerves! Nerves! She's a bundle of nerves!"

But Debbie was delivered of the demon of nerves and she no longer bites her nails.

4. MANY DEMONS CAN LIVE IN A PERSON
AT THE SAME TIME

There are several examples of multiple possession in the Bible. The spirits in the Gadarene man identified themselves as "Legion, for we are many." (A legion was a Roman military unit which comprised anywhere from 3,000 to 6,000 soldiers.)

Mary Magdalene was delivered of seven demons, and Jesus described a man to whom an unclean spirit returned bringing seven others, a total of eight.

The largest number I personally have ever encountered in a single person was forty-one. One night at the Musselman home, a woman who had several times experienced deliverance there confessed to having had a struggle during the day and asked that we minister to her once more. Two spirits were identified and cast out. She commented, "That makes forty spirits that I have been delivered of in recent weeks, but I feel there is still one more."

Again we addressed any spirit still lodged within her. Suddenly she began to sniffle. I commanded the spirit to identify itself and a tiny, tearful voice spoke out of the woman.

"I'm here all alone! Don't you understand? All alone! I just can't do all this work by myself!"

At last the spirit whimpered out its name: "laziness," and, still grumbling, the forty-first demon came out.

5. DEMONS ARE FILTHY

On the Judy tape, David Lawson used the word "gagging" to describe what happened during Judy's deliverance. I glanced over the list I myself had drawn up of physical manifestations at the moment a demon was expelled—most of them equally distasteful.

Why was it that encounters with Satan's world so often included such side effects?

Could it be because, here, Satan was showing his true nature? Suddenly I saw in a new way the revolting side of some deliverances. This was what Satan was really like: vile! From that moment on, when faced with the repellent moments of this ministry, instead of being put off I was going to thank God that I was getting a clearer look at the enemy.

A vivid and unforgettable illustration of this occurred one day when I was visiting Jack Herd, a chiropractor who lives in Harrisburg, Pennsylvania. During my stay we ministered deliverance in Jack's home to a young man named Jim. One evil spirit proved most stubborn. Its name was "insanity" and it screamed and raged and swore. As we gave the repeated command for the demon to come out, Jim fell on the floor and began to retch. All at once he brought up a quantity of mucouslike material. While Jack Herd's poor wife cleaned up the mess on the rug in one spot, Jim continued to be sick in another. Then to our shock and dismay, Jim lunged free from our grasp, thrust his face directly into the vomit and began to eat it. As we dragged him away the demon within him began to scream: "Leave me alone! Can't you see I *have* to eat this? It's my life, I tell you! It's my very life!"

The true picture of the devil! He's foul! Even his New Testament name, Beelzebub, "Lord of the Flies," signifies a carrier of filthy things.

6. DEMONS ARE NOT TO BE FEARED IN CHRIST

The sum of these qualities was clear to me; in observing Satan's strength, his desire to destroy, his true ugliness, I began to see what I was up against in this new ministry. And I must admit it sobered me. Who was I to deal with such a formidable foe?

And yet, wasn't it extraordinary! Jesus had sent you and me

out to do battle with this very Satan, and all his myriad host. How was this possible when I knew so well my own weaknesses, my susceptibility to his wiles?

Then one day I glimpsed the answer to these fears. I read in Scripture that Satan was the "father of lies." All that he says to us is a lie! All his claims are based on lies. How often the temptations of demons seem attractive to us; but we see in the retching what their real nature is. How often we have been deceived into believing that certain problems cannot be overcome. Yet we are seeing daily that people *can* be set free! Free from years-old compulsions, emotions, habits, weaknesses.

Satan's vaunted power to steal, kill, and destroy is based on a lie: the lie that he is still in command. But we know the truth and we must proclaim that truth in the Church. The truth is that Satan is a defeated foe, conquered once and for all on Calvary by the One who loved us before the foundation of the world.

In Luke, chapter ten, is the account of Jesus appointing seventy disciples and sending them out, two by two, to minister in the towns and cities He himself will visit later. During their journey the seventy discover the reality of the deliverance ministry and return rejoicing: "Lord, even the devils are subject unto us through Thy name!"

"I beheld Satan as lightning fall from heaven," Jesus answers. And then He gives us the marching orders which dispel our fears:

"Behold, I give unto you power to tread on serpents and scorpions, and *over all the power of the enemy;* and nothing shall by any means hurt you."

12

Meeting the Conditions

BUT knowing that Satan and his demons are defeated is one thing: appropriating the benefits of that defeat is quite another. The more I was thrown into this strange ministry, the more complex it seemed to become. Why, for example, should deliverance achieve such spectacular results in one tormented person and fail miserably with another? Gradually I began to see that there were certain contributing factors, certain requirements or conditions for deliverance. To a large degree success was determined by whether or not the one seeking help was willing to meet the conditions. It was almost as if I could divide the people needing deliverance into two groups: the reluctant and the ready. Over a considerable period of time I compiled a list of these conditions.

1. *The person must desire deliverance.*

One day I was ministering in Kansas City when a man spoke to me of a problem he was having with alcohol. He described how, periodically, usually when he was away from home, he would go on an enormous bender. "I always drink rather heavily," he said, "but when I'm on a trip, I just plain get drunk." As the man

147

continued to describe his behavior, the compulsive quality of it did indeed suggest a demon.

"And you think it may be a demon that won't let you give up drinking?" I asked.

"Give it up!" the man was aghast. "Whoever said that? No, no, I just want to be able to keep it within reason. I'm not an alcoholic. I just overdo it on occasion, that's all."

When I explained that anyone whose drinking had opened the door to a demon would, after deliverance, have to keep that door firmly shut, he turned and walked away.

Later, I realized that this man had simply admitted openly what many people who claimed they wanted deliverance felt. They wanted to retain their habit patterns, but on a less destructive scale. Why? Obviously because our various captivities are not always unpleasant. Certain crutches—even though they lead us into dependence—are functional: they help us escape some unpleasant reality. True freedom entails responsibility, and responsibility is not always welcome: the Israelites longed to go back to Egypt.

But the fact that people may not desire freedom is often overlooked by friends who want help for them. One night in a high school in Buffalo, New York, I spoke to a gathering of about three hundred Christians, mostly Roman Catholic, on the theme of the charismatic renewal, including the deliverance ministry. At the encouragement of the priest I agreed to remain after the meeting to pray with people.

Some teen-age girls, he said, wanted help for a friend of theirs who, they felt, needed deliverance from an uncontrollable habit of cursing. They introduced me to her, a heavy-set, sullen-faced girl wearing an Indian headband, a Snoopy T-shirt, and dungarees. Somewhat reluctantly she admitted that she had accepted Christ and that, yes, she was willing to be prayed for.

But as we prayed, she became increasingly sullen. A demon of profanity was identified but before we could cast it out she suddenly jumped to her feet.

"I don't want you praying for me! I don't know why I agreed to come here! Just leave me alone! You're all a bunch of idiots and I want you to leave me alone!" Shoving her friends aside she dashed out of the gymnasium.

When the meeting finally closed and I left the building I saw her sitting disconsolately on the school steps. I started to speak to her but she swore at me and walked away. It seemed apparent that her friends had been more eager for her deliverance than she herself had been.

2. *The person must be willing to admit that he has a demon.*

At the altar of a Pentecostal church in Jacksonville, Florida, one night I was still ministering to a man long after the meeting had ended and everyone else had gone home. Several spirits were identified and cast out, but the deliverance was proving slow and difficult. Resistance within the man himself seemed to be stiffening.

Finally, after repeated and stern commands for a spirit to identify itself, a name emerged. Through clenched teeth came the word, "nicotine," spoken against much inner opposition. Immediately the man protested: "But that can't be an evil spirit! There's nothing wrong with smoking and I don't see why I should give it up."

And that ended the session.

An even more dramatic instance occurred in Atlanta, Georgia. I was in the home of Dr. Ray Coombes and his wife, Lucy. Ray is an ophthalmologist; with his scientific training I half expected resistance to the concept of demons to come from him. Actually it was his wife Lucy who stumbled over the idea. During a meeting earlier that evening where I had spoken on deliverance Lucy had seemed unhappy. Later at their home, every move and gesture reflected her opposition to the subject. She listened to our continuing discussion with increasingly apparent annoyance. All at once she burst out, "I don't believe any of that stuff! Do you two realize it's after midnight? I think we should all go to bed!" Before we could respond to her angry outburst, she looked at me imploringly. "Don, I'm so sorry for the way I'm acting. I don't think I've ever been this rude in my whole life."

"It's all right, Lucy," I assured her. "What do you think is making you act in a way you don't choose?"

"A demon?"

"I'm asking you."

"But it's such an ugly thought!" she protested. "I don't want even to admit the possibility!" Finally realizing her very opposition could be an indication that she needed deliverance, with a tremendous surge of the will she asked Ray and me to pray for her.

It was three o'clock before we got to bed that night, but seeing Lucy set free from resentments and hatreds which had plagued her since childhood was worth it. Later she wrote me a letter describing her reactions:

I knew something wasn't right, and I had tried every way I knew to get victory over the problems, yet nothing worked. Frankly, I'd secretly decided that everyone else was in the same boat, but wouldn't admit it. We all know what we are supposed to be. You know—pretending to have something we really don't have. I had reached the point where I was continually impatient with the children. I cried many times over the way I acted with them. I hated myself for it, but I did it anyway.

I heard about the deliverance ministry and decided this might be my problem. But then, when you came that night and we talked about deliverance here in the house, I found *I was aghast at the possibility of having a demon.*

But now I just can't tell you the feeling of gratitude to the Lord which I have. I enjoy being with the children again, and being a wife to Ray. Pardon me while I leap for joy.

3. *Those ministering deliverance must take authority in the name of Jesus.*

The more experience I gained in this area the more I came to see the significance of Jesus' statement in Mark 16:17: *"In my name* shall they cast out devils . . . ."* I came to appreciate as never before the mighty spiritual authority in that name. On numerous occasions I have actually heard the evil spirit speak through the lips of the person it inhabited to curse the name of Jesus. Other times the demons would cry out, saying, "Stop using that name! We can't stand to hear the name of Jesus! It torments us." Such strange happenings made me all the more aware that it is Jesus' own ministry of deliverance that we are participating in.

Smith-Wigglesworth tells in *Ever-Increasing Faith* about the deliverance of a young girl: "As I went into the room the evil powers looked out of her eyes and they used her lips, saying, 'We are many, you can't cast us out.' I said, 'Jesus can . . . .' "

It is not we who are stronger than Satan, it is Jesus Christ. And even this is not the whole story. Jesus has the strength; it is we who must utilize that strength. To the seventy He said, "Behold, I give unto *you* power . . . over all the power of the enemy." [Luke 10:19] It is Jesus' power; it is we who move in it. When we come against demonic forces in His name, we are fulfilling His mission on earth. To pray in Jesus' name is actually to minister by the power and authority that name provides. Describing the deliverance of the young girl, Smith-Wigglesworth adds: "There is power in the name of Jesus. His name, through faith in his name, brought deliverance to this poor bound soul, and thirty-seven demons came out, giving their names as they came forth."

4. *It helps to get the demon to name itself.*

Going hand in hand with the role of Jesus' name is the role played by the name of the evil spirit itself. In most cases of deliverance I have found it helpful to have the spirit identify itself. At first I was unsure why this naming was so important; quickly I came to realize two things. First, from the standpoint of the person who needs deliverance, naming the spirit proves an exercise in honesty. I am likely to give polite names to my weaknesses. I have a "roving eye" but the spirit names itself as *lust*. I "eat a little too much" but the spirit calls itself *gluttony*. The person honest enough to pinpoint and admit his torment meets an essential prerequisite for deliverance.

Second, from time immeasurable people have felt that a name reflects the essence of the person named. Simon was Simon until he became so changed that Jesus gave him the new name, Peter. Jacob became Israel after a life-changing crisis. In a name lies the central character of the named. To get a demon to name itself is to get it to reveal its essential nature. I found that demons, when commanded in Jesus' name to identify themselves, although they might protest and argue, when pressed had to obey.

The noticeable reluctance of some evil spirits to comply with the command is, itself, an indication of the importance of the technique. While ministering to a young woman in Washington, D.C., I commanded the spirit to identify itself.

"Leave me alone," the demon snarled out through the girl's lips. "I will not tell you my name."

I was pretty sure we were dealing with a spirit of lust: sure enough, every time the young woman tried to say the word "lust" she choked. Repeatedly the demon refused to allow the girl to speak its name and a struggle of some five minutes ensued before the girl could exercise her own will over her vocal cords.

Naming the spirit brings the thing to light, and since all evil thrives in deception and darkness and hates the truth and the light, naming the spirit exposes it, weakens its hold, and sets the stage for deliverance.

5. *The afflicted person must renounce the demon.*

It was the difficulties I encountered in this ministry which seemed to teach me the most, and in one such difficult situation I learned the importance of renunciation.

Angela Gigliano was a handsome woman in her mid-fifties who had lived in South America as an executive in a cosmetics firm before returning home to live in Miami Beach. Through friends she became interested in the charismatic renewal and attended a seminar in a hotel where I was talking about deliverance. Afterward she drew me aside.

"I'm not sure what it is," she said. "But something inside me was trembling violently the whole time you spoke."

Finding chairs in the rear of the conference room we began to pray. Mrs. Gigliano's trembling increased and suddenly the spirit agitating her identified itself.

"You know," she said, "the word 'witchcraft' keeps popping into my mind."

And indeed when I commanded the spirit of witchcraft to leave, Mrs. Gigliano's face grew red and her eyes began to bulge as if someone were tightening a noose around her neck. Every time I gave the command, her distress seemed to increase.

"Please stop," she finally gasped. "I can hardly breathe!"

Frustrated and baffled I sought some clue to breaking the demon's stubbornness. Why wasn't it yielding to the power of Jesus' name? *Was it because He will never impose His will on our wills?* Could it be that Mrs. Gigliano had not fulfilled the very first condition? That in some subconscious part of herself she did not *want* to be delivered? "How do you suppose that spirit got hold of you in the first place?" I asked. "You've never practiced witchcraft, have you?"

Mrs. Gigliano's reply was curt. "Of course not." Then, more gently, she added, "But one of my servants did."

"One of your servants?"

"Yes. When we lived in South America one of my maids boasted openly of being a witch. I used to get these terrible headaches. Marianna would put funny little dolls and charms under my pillow, and the headaches would go away. I was glad of anything that worked. I saw no harm in it then—but maybe I was playing on a double team and didn't know it."

And it was then that I glimpsed a stage beyond the simple desire for deliverance, a step of active, aggressive opposition to any satanic agent lodging within us. "Did you ever resign from that team?" I asked her.

"What do you mean?"

"I think you were glad enough to get rid of the headaches that you are still holding on to some favorable memory of the experience. Perhaps you need to disavow all association with that realm."

"How do I do that?"

"By confessing it to God as sin."

Mrs. Gigliano bowed her head. "Dear Father in heaven, I'm sorry I got mixed up with Marianna and her witchcraft. Please forgive me. Amen." She raised her eyes and looked at me. "I don't think it helped much."

"But you just confessed your involvement. You didn't really take a stand *against* witchcraft. Why not make it stronger: 'In the name of Jesus, I renounce anything to do with witchcraft.' "

Mrs. Gigliano opened her mouth to speak but no words came. She took a deep breath and tried again.

"In . . . the . . . name . . ."

I leaned forward, "Try again, I think we're onto something."

"In . . . the . . . name . . . of Je . . . Je . . ." Drops of perspiration appeared on her face from the force of her effort. She made one final effort.

"In . . . the . . . name . . . of Jesus . . . I . . . renounce witchcraft." Immediately her breathing became easier.

Realizing that this prayer of renunciation must have been extremely important or the demon would not have exerted so much resistance, I said, "Repeat your renunciation again several times for emphasis."

Mrs. Gigliano complied, her voice growing stronger and clearer every time she said the words.

Then once more I spoke to the spirit. "You demon of witchcraft, you are renounced. I command you to come *out* in the name of Jesus."

This time Mrs. Gigliano rose from her chair, her head thrown back. From her mouth came the drawn-out wail I knew so well, then she collapsed back onto the seat breathing with relief.

6. *The person must forgive.*

A pastor for nearly fifteen years, I had encountered many situations in counseling where forgiveness was essential. But it was not until God thrust me into the deliverance ministry that I came to see the stark necessity for this Christian virtue. Jesus stated it most simply in Matthew 6:15: ". . . if you forgive not men their trespasses, neither will your Father forgive your trespasses." I was to discover that lack of forgiveness was perhaps the largest single contributor to demonic bondage. And, as usual, I had to learn it by difficulties encountered in my ministry.

Max had been a marine and had rarely been out of trouble since his discharge. He had taken up bartending, had fallen in with some rough characters, and ended up serving three years in prison for armed robbery. Then came his conversion.

But even after this, he was still subject to fits of violent anger. He talked of having lost many jobs because of fights he would get into.

So I explained a little about the ministry of deliverance and then we prayed together. "Thoughts of violence just spilled over in my mind the minute you started praying," Max confessed. "So the name of the spirit must be: violence."

When I commanded the spirit of violence to come out Max began to feel physical discomfort, which he described as a pain in his chest. At my suggestion he tried coughing to expel it, but said he had no sensation of anything coming out.

After half an hour Max was no nearer being free than when we started. No matter how many times he renounced the spirit, no matter how firmly I commanded it to leave, Max's tormentor remained.

"I can't understand why the thing won't turn you loose, Max," I finally admitted, feeling the same weary frustration I had felt on previous occasions when I had prayed and nothing had happened.

And then God stepped in.

As Max continued to renounce the demon of violence I found myself silently asking Jesus for help. Suddenly I had a vivid impression of Max as a boy of about ten, screaming hysterically at his mother, pounding at her with his fists. The image remained in my mind for only a few seconds, then it was gone.

One of the gifts of the Holy Spirit mentioned in I Corinthians 12 is the word of Knowledge, the mystic imparting of information to be used in carrying out Jesus' work on earth. My heart skipped a beat. Could it be that I was experiencing this gift right now? Could it be that in fact God was giving me a piece of information which would be helpful in Max's delivery?

"Max," I said, "let me ask you something. When you were a boy of—say—nine or ten, did something happen between you and your mother which caused you to stop loving her?"

Max's mouth fell open and his face turned ashen. "Why, how . . . how did you know that?" he stammered. Then he buried his face in his hands and began to sob.

"I hate her. Oh, how I hate her," he wailed between sobs. "When I was ten she deserted me and my father. Just ran off. I hate her!" For a full minute he sobbed uncontrollably. Then the weeping subsided and wiping his tear-streaked face with his handkerchief he stared at me strangely. "But how in the world could you have known that? I haven't talked about it to a soul, not in years!"

"Jesus showed me, Max," I replied. "That proves how much He wants to help you. He gave me a picture of you as a boy screaming and striking at your mother. Did you ever have these violent outbursts *before* your mother deserted you?"

Max thought for a minute before answering. Finally he shook his head. "No, in fact the very first time was the day she told us she was leaving."

"Then this must have been the point when the spirit of violence entered. I don't think that spirit will come out, Max, until you forgive your mother."

"Forgive her!" Max growled. "After what she did? Never." He leaned toward me. "Listen," he said, "when I became a Christian I tried to forgive everyone who ever treated me dirty. I forgave the girl who jilted me and married another guy while I was overseas. I forgave the prison guard who beat me with a rubber hose. But this thing with my mother goes too deep. I won't forgive her!"

Suddenly I saw a way to help Max with his own words.

"Did you hear what you just said?" I asked him.

"What do you mean?"

"You said, I *won't* forgive my mother."

"So what?"

"Don't you see, Max, the word 'won't' is a contraction of 'will not.' You just said you *will* not forgive your mother. You have willed—decided—not to forgive her. It was a choice you made. But if you chose *not* to forgive her, you can also choose *to* forgive her. It lies not with your emotions but with your will."

Max frowned for a minute. "I think I'm beginning to see what you mean," he said at last. It took another half-hour of battling, but finally Max bowed his head and said a simple prayer: "In the name of Jesus Christ I do will to forgive my mother for deserting me and my father." It must have been a tremendous effort. Max remained silent for a minute, head still bowed, breathing heavily. "In the name of Jesus I *do* forgive my mother. Thank you Lord for helping me."

Then before I could say anything further, he doubled over and coughed, this time in earnest.

"I don't know why I did that," he said looking at me in surprise. Then he put his hand on his chest. "Hey," he exclaimed, "the pain is gone! I can breathe!"

And indeed Max's deliverance had occurred without a further word from either of us. So all-changing was that act of forgiveness that the demon, its long-time dwelling place destroyed, fled in the very same instant.

13

Keeping Our Deliverance

ONE morning a woman called on Alice and me at our house seeking help. While Alice served us coffee in the living room, this middle-aged lady told me that she had recently suffered a nervous breakdown, followed by confinement in a hospital. When she left the hospital the doctor put her on tranquilizers. She had become so accustomed to them that she could not, now, face day-to-day tensions without her daily dosage.

"It's this emotional dependency that bothers me," she said. "A friend has been following your work and she suggests that this may be demonic. What do you think?"

"I don't know," I answered. "I've never heard of a demon of tranquilizers but I certainly doubt that any chemical dependency could be of the Lord. Would you like to pray about it?"

As we prayed, a spirit of addiction named itself. It was still, no matter how often we saw it, a remarkable thing to witness the transformation which took place under the deliverance ministry.

Right there at our coffee table Alice and I watched the strained and tormented expression leave this woman's face. She looked years younger. When she left I was satisfied that she had been greatly helped.

Two weeks later, though, I met our mutual friend. "How's Adelaide?" I asked.

The friend shook her head sadly. "She's having trouble again, and she's angry with you."

"What happened?"

So the story came out. Adelaide had been absolutely free for about eight days after her deliverance. She had lived those days in a kind of heavenly peace. No nervousness, no fear, and no desire for drugs. Then one night Adelaide's husband came home intoxicated. It was a realistic point of tension and Adelaide took a couple of tranquilizers. By the next week she was taking tranquilizers regularly again. Long after the trauma of the drunken husband had passed she was still plagued with such tensions as to "require" chemical solution.

"How do you account for it?" our friend asked.

How indeed? Nor was it the first time the question had come up; I was running into the problem with increasing frequency.

Most people who were delivered seemed to stay delivered; often I would hear heart-warming reports of their continued victory and freedom. But more and more I was encountering those who—like Adelaide—seemed initially helped, only to suffer a relapse.

One day shortly after the experience with Adelaide, I had a long-distance phone call from Maxwell Whyte in Toronto.

"Don," he asked, "did you minister to a former parishioner of mine named Williams, your last time in Detroit?"

Indeed I had. In a small Methodist church Mrs. Williams, along with several other people, had come to the altar for prayer for healing. There had been no mention of deliverance in my message; nevertheless, when I laid hands on Mrs. Williams's head she had begun to wail incoherently. The minister took her into his office where we prayed for her deliverance with startling effectiveness. The pastor was at first stunned, then amazed, and finally elated over the dramatic change in his parishioner.

"Yes, I did," I answered. "How did you hear about it?" I was feeling a little prideful over her deliverance and was completely unprepared for Maxwell Whyte's next words.

"Mrs. Williams phoned me at two this morning." His voice was wry. "She was nearly hysterical. Said the demons had come back and she was worse than she'd ever been."

I was dismayed. "I'm sorry she picked on you," I apologized. "But I don't understand. I felt sure her deliverance was real. What do you suppose I did wrong?"

Maxwell Whyte gave a sympathetic chuckle over the telephone. "I doubt you did anything wrong. She didn't protect her deliverance and the demons came back, that's all."

Protect her deliverance? Could this have been Adelaide's problem too?

I turned to my Bible once more. And as I examined the problem in the light of Scripture I saw a truth I had glimpsed only faintly before: *Man has a vital role to play in keeping any healing which God brings to his life.*

For example, to the lame man healed on the Sabbath, Jesus gave sober advice: "See, you are well! Sin no more, that nothing worse befall you." [John 5:14 RSV]

And concerning deliverance He warned that "seven other spirits more evil than the first" *could* enter a man who had been delivered, making his last state worse than his first (Matthew 12:45). It seemed a strange and troubling saying, as if implying that to be delivered from an evil spirit was risky, opening the door to still worse torment.

But then I saw that Jesus was simply saying that we must protect what God has given us. The evil spirit in Jesus' teaching returned to find his house swept, yes; and put in order, too; but it was empty. The man had done nothing to fill up his "house" with the Holy Spirit so that the evil spirit could not find room. The implication, at any rate, was that instead of making a definite move toward God, the man had continued in his old way, leaving himself wide open for reinvasion by the enemy.

I found myself thinking of an analogy Derek Prince had used one evening when Alice and I heard him speak at the Holy Spirit Teaching Mission in Fort Lauderdale. Recalling Paul's statement about "spiritual warfare," he likened the human personality to a great city made up of different neighborhoods. Conquest of the whole city is Satan's ultimate aim. The person in need of deliverance is like a city with some neighborhoods which have already been captured, and are under the control of the enemy.

In the deliverance ministry, said Derek, we "storm the city" to drive the enemy out. In the process some of the city walls are destroyed. After the invader has gone, rebuilding must take place, defenses must be restored.

In addition, occupied districts often lose the initiative to care for themselves. So it is in Derek's illustration with areas that have been occupied by demons. After the demons are cast out, he cautioned, the person must reassume control of those areas of his personality where the demons resided.

Some people, apparently, did this automatically. Others, like Adelaide and Mrs. Williams, would need guidance and support in "rebuilding the walls." It all seemed so clear and so essential that I regretted I had not been teaching these things all along.

The basic answer to keeping what God gives us, I knew, whether it's salvation, healing or deliverance, is *total commitment of one's life to Jesus Christ*. In practice, of course, this must be worked out in the specifics of daily living. Over the next few weeks I listed some of these specifics.

Total Commitment to Jesus Christ

1. Live by the Scriptures
2. Learn to praise God continually
3. Protect and guard your thought life
4. Cultivate right relationships
5. Submit to discipline

For the person who has received deliverance, these steps will be of critical importance. Total commitment to Jesus Christ means that with a voluntary act of the will every area of life is to be surrendered to the Lordship of Jesus Christ. No more partial commitments. Such a surrender recognizes the right of Christ to control and govern each decision as it arises.

1. LIVE BY THE SCRIPTURES

The word of God proclaims Satan's defeat. By standing on God's word, a person who has been delivered can block Satan's attempts to return. Jesus himself, during His temptations, withstood Satan by reliance on the written word. "It is written . . ." he said in response to every allurement of the devil. The Scriptures confirm that health, protection, and deliverance are all part of our inheritance in Christ. But we cannot claim these promises if we are not aware of them—and this means prayerful and expectant daily Bible reading.

2. LEARN TO PRAISE GOD CONTINUALLY

"The devil never has much luck with a grateful man." An attitude of thanksgiving and praise can thwart Satan's efforts to dislodge us from our place in Christ. Such an attitude is especially important after deliverance: it is one of the ways we "rebuild the walls." "Rejoice evermore," Paul wrote the Thessalonians, and "in every thing give thanks: for this is the will of God in Christ Jesus concerning you."

3. PROTECT AND GUARD YOUR THOUGHT LIFE

The mind is Satan's primary target. By suggestion and insinuation his temptations subtly begin. Therefore we must "put on the *helmet* of salvation" to cover and protect the mind. This means nipping certain conversations in the bud; it means avoiding certain films, books, and environments that we know spell danger for us. It is no sin to be tempted, but to invite and entertain temptation is to hold open a door to the enemy.

4. CULTIVATE RIGHT RELATIONSHIPS

Hatred and resentment toward others creates the ideal climate for demonic invasion. Just as a person can scarcely be delivered without forgiving those who have injured him, neither can he keep his deliverance for long if he permits bitterness and resentment to creep back in. Maintaining loving relationships with others and practicing continual on-the-spot forgiveness are two of the surest wall-builders.

5. SUBMIT TO DISCIPLINE

Demonic problems are often the result of overindulgence of some appetite or weakness of the flesh. For the one delivered, discipline becomes an essential part of keeping the victory. Not just self-discipline but also submission to others more mature in Jesus Christ. This means becoming a part of a regularly meeting body of Christians and submitting our plans and desires to the wisdom of the group.

Some time after drawing up this list I had the chance to minister to Adelaide again and this time I passed on to her the five basic steps for maintaining deliverance. Adelaide promised that she would try to follow them; we hear from her from time to time and the principles seem to be working.

I don't mean to indicate that she has no problems. In fact, her husband eventually lost his job because of his trouble with alcohol. But I can state that Adelaide has remained free of the demon which had been plaguing her. She faces her problems now without the added burden of drug dependence.

From that time on, when I ministered deliverance, I also encouraged people to take definite steps to protect what God had given them. Sure enough, complaints about demons returning began to diminish. It wasn't until later that I came to see another subtle tactic of Satan in his efforts to rob us of our victories.

I met John in Cleveland, Ohio. A Presbyterian pastor, John had a thriving church where the charismatic movement was active and healthy. Still, he himself had a personal problem which he had not been able to overcome.

"I tell you frankly, Don," John told me one sunny afternoon as we drove along Lake Erie, "I don't think *this* makes a very good witness." And he patted his huge stomach. It was true: John was very badly overweight. He described a lifelong struggle against overeating. "It's not glandular, it's not a medical problem. It's simply a case of too many calories," John confessed. "I know that but I can't seem to do anything about it. Listening to your talk about demons, I began to wonder if I am being manipulated by some kind of spirit. Do you think we could pray about it together?"

Of course we could. We pulled into a parking area overlooking the lake and I led John step by step through deliverance. As we both expected, gluttony was identified and cast out. Afterward I gave John some suggestions on protecting his deliverance. As far as I could tell we had left nothing undone to ensure John the victory he so earnestly desired. By now I had witnessed so many deliverances I would have stated confidently that this was a successful one.

I make such a point of this because three months later when I was in Cleveland again I looked forward to seeing John. But it became obvious that he was making every effort to avoid me. When we finally appeared at the same meeting together I saw why: if anything John was heavier than before. After the meeting I approached him.

"Something is wrong between me and thee," I said. "Can we talk about it?"

John looked at me for a long time, then finally nodded. "Yes there is something wrong. This deliverance business of yours just doesn't work . . . as you can see."

John's story was most interesting. After his deliverance he had had two weeks of freedom from his old compulsion to open the refrigerator door every time he passed it. He was delighted and went about telling people of the tremendous gift God had given him. During this short period he did indeed lose ten pounds.

But then, bit by bit, it became difficult again for him to pass that refrigerator. John was confused. If indeed he had been delivered how could he still be having his old problem?

"I can understand how healing can be a process," John said. "You can become well bit by bit. But deliverance is different, isn't it? Either you have a demon or you don't. I guess my demon of gluttony never left. Or if it did, it came back."

As I listened I suddenly caught Satan in the middle of a lie. I recalled from my earlier research how both evil spirits and the carnal nature were concerns of the New Testament church. The first Christians used deliverance if the problem was evil spirits, prayer and self-discipline to crucify the flesh. That, I suddenly saw, could be the answer to John's difficulty. He was involved not with one problem, but two. When John was young he had a tendency "in the flesh" to overeat. It was a weakness to be overcome by prayer and will power. But subtly and cleverly an evil spirit took advantage of this weakness and invaded his body as a demon of gluttony. Then John had two forces to contend with; his natural tendency to eat too much, and an evil spirit which had taken root in this weakness and lived there.

I explained the principle to John.

"Don't you see," I said to him. "You really were set free from the evil spirit which had been tormenting you. What was left was the natural ground, your own liking for food. The demon you could not control, but your own appetite you can. Remember, an evil spirit comes in through our weakness. After it is cast out, we still have the weakness to overcome."

I saw the light of understanding come into John's eyes.

"Don, I do believe you are right!" he exclaimed. "I was so excited with my deliverance and freedom those first few days that I completely forgot my natural craving for food. When some of that craving returned I guess I became discouraged and assumed nothing had happened."

"Then go back to your victory," I said to John. "Claim it again. What you are encountering now is simply a temptation of the flesh and you can control it. It's not the spirit of gluttony still in control, and don't let the devil tell you it is."

I saw John again some months later. It was, frankly, a bit difficult to recognize him. He had lost sixty pounds. His skin tone was firm, his step light.

"Ah, there you are," John said with mock severity. "I've got a score to settle with you. Do you realize that you and your deliverance ministry have cost me an entire wardrobe?"

14

Mistakes, Mistakes

WHEN I got home from Cleveland I found a letter from Ray and Lucy Coombes. Lucy had shared the story of her deliverance with the prayer group which met in their home; almost before they knew it, they found *themselves* ministering deliverance to others with problems. I was delighted: the Lord needed many Ray and Lucy Coombeses! One sentence in the letter challenged me particularly.

> When you were here you mentioned making various mistakes as you started out in deliverance. Would you mind jotting some of them down and sending them to us? With luck, we might be able to avoid making the same ones.

That same afternoon I sat down at my desk in the kitchen and began to evaluate my own ministry, recalling various mistakes I had made and was making as I moved ahead in the deliverance ministry.

1. *When I started out I was so enthusiastic that I forced the subject on people.*

My friend Charles Simpson caught me at this one. When I first grasped the reality of deliverance I began to see a demon behind every human misery. "That sounds like it might be a demon" was a sentence on my lips far too frequently. Charles was minister of the Bayview Heights Baptist Church in Mobile, Alabama, and in demand nationwide as a Bible teacher. At a convention in Washington, D.C., where I had been particularly insistent in my remarks about deliverance, Charles said to me quietly, "Don, you realize, don't you, that you don't have to go around shouting 'demon'?"

It was all I needed. For a little while, as I learned about the deliverance ministry I knew I would have to focus my attention on it. This is the nature of any new study; you have to put everything else from your mind while you try to understand. But I determined, after Charles's comment, to see deliverance in its proper place, as only one of the ministries of Jesus. I knew from my study of the Scriptures that Jesus' ministry had been divided into four major thrusts. Besides coming as Savior, he was also Healer, Baptizer in the Holy Spirit, and Deliverer. For centuries the Church had emphasized only His first role. Now the Holy Spirit was reminding us of the other three. And it was up to us to accept and place each function in its proper perspective; as an essential part—but *only* a part—of Christ's total ministry. Like healing and the baptism in the Holy Spirit, deliverance had been almost totally left out of the Church's life for many years. Once reinstated, it should assume normal proportions.

2. *I had a tendency at first to promise a kind of "instant sainthood" through deliverance.*

When I first saw that evil spirits were real and could torment us, and that people could be delivered from such torment, I fell into the trap of thinking that deliverance was the ultimate answer to all the Church's problems. All we had to do was say a few quick words of exorcism and every problem disappeared.

Well, it just doesn't work that simply.

The problems that beset our planet are many and varied—everything from earthquake, famine, and plague to individual weaknesses of physique, body chemistry, emotional makeup. The great social, economic, and ecological crises of our day are likewise the Church's crises, and there are no shortcut solutions.

Even when a particular problem is traceable to demon activity, there is nothing automatic about the solution. We bear the responsibility both for meeting the conditions of deliverance and for keeping it once it is ours. And of course each of us has the "old man" battle to fight. Deliverance has nothing to do with the continuing battle we must fight against the willfulness of the old self as we "work out our own salvation in fear and trembling." This was the truth my minister friend John, in Cleveland, discovered.

3. *I failed to remember the slow, protesting route over which God had led me, and at times barged in with deliverance where people weren't ready.*

I was ignoring the scriptural principle of "first the blade, then the ear, then the full corn in the ear." After I spoke in one Episcopal church in Virginia, only a single parishioner came forward. "I'm sure I need help," the woman said, kneeling in front of the altar. And she received it. Spirit after spirit was identified and cast out, to her great joy and gratitude.

During her deliverance, however, I noticed that the rector of the church was giving us a wide berth; he escaped to the back of the sanctuary, later disappeared altogether. Several of the congregation also left abruptly when the deliverance started. When I had finished, a member of the vestry came up to me and spoke in an embarrassed manner.

"Mr. Basham, nothing in your correspondence mentioned that you were into this—ah, sort of thing. *Did you tell our rector what you were going to speak about?*"

"Well, uh—no, I didn't."

"I see." The man's voice was dismayed. "Then you spoke on deliverance without his permission?"

I felt my face turning red as I realized I had assumed a right I did not have. After all, the minister knew the needs of his people far better than I did.

"I personally believe in this ministry," the vestryman added, surprisingly. "And I think something important happened with Mrs. Horton tonight. But I'm afraid you've created some problems for our rector. You'll be on your way tomorrow, but he must remain and minister to all the people who were not yet ready to hear the message you gave tonight."

4. *I made the mistake of taking too much of the burden of deliverance onto myself.*

In any work undertaken for God, the more you can get yourself out of the way, the more effective the ministry. While I knew this to be true in this area too, nevertheless in practice I would repeatedly interject myself into it. If the deliverance proved to be a noisy one, with the demons talking back or crying out, I often found myself tensing and yelling back, as if by speaking in a loud voice I could exercise greater authority. At home after such a service I would find Alice shaking her head sympathetically. "You've been in deliverance again, haven't you?"

"How do you know?"

"Because you've yelled yourself hoarse."

I had to come to the point of remembering, as I began each deliverance service, that the spiritual authority rests solely in the name of Jesus Christ and not in any histrionics of mine.

5. *I would also get involved in deliverance services lasting for hours, draining myself beyond reason.*

Even though the deliverance ministry is accomplished by the power of Jesus, that power must be transmitted through Christians with physical limitations. Jesus himself in His earthly life knew what it was to grow tired.

I will never forget the night, for instance, when I came to see the literal meaning of Paul's statement in Ephesians that "we wrestle not against flesh and blood, but against principalities, against powers . . . ." While on vacation in North Carolina, Alice and I were attending a house prayer meeting. We had gone only to worship, not to minister. Nevertheless, during the meeting a young woman who had suffered a nervous breakdown grew distraught and friends asked us to minister to her. The battle lasted for four hours, and over thirty different spirits were identified and cast out. By the end of the session the young woman was free, but I was physically and spiritually exhausted.

But as luck would have it, as I staggered out of the family room sometime after 1:00 A.M. I was met by two other troubled people insisting on ministry. They claimed the Lord had shown them they were to be delivered that very night. Foolishly I tried to minister to them, even though I felt God was saying no. Little was accomplished and after another two hours I was almost ready to collapse. There is a definite limit to the amount the physical body can stand. I had to learn my own limit and to honor it.

6. *At first I had a tendency to panic when Satan counterattacked by harassing me or my family.*

One night after a particularly successful deliverance · service I had a nightmare which seemed almost childish, yet which terrified me. A ghoulish figure seemed to stand at the foot of my bed with a gray shroud over its head moaning and gesticulating. Even through the strange terror it aroused in me I recognized the sounds and gestures as Grade-C movie stuff.

"In Jesus' name I command you to leave me alone!" I cried aloud, waking both Alice and myself.

"What is it, hon?" Alice asked.

"Just a stupid nightmare," I sighed. "Go back to sleep."

Alice's breathing became soft and regular once more but I lay awake until daylight lest the thing haunt my sleep again. Later, pondering and praying over the incident, noting that it had come right on the heels of a successful effort at deliverance, I realized that it had been an essentially harmless episode, and that such happenings could affect me only if I took them more seriously than I needed to.

But I also had to learn to take the same attitude toward Satan's harassment of Alice and the children, and that wasn't quite so easy. Until the day when Satan overplayed his hand.

I was sitting at my desk in the kitchen making some notes on a deliverance message I was to teach at the Musselmans' meeting that night. I had just written these words: "A favorite tactic of Satan to discourage the deliverance ministry is to harass members of your family." I was actually writing the words as Alice, with Laura standing beside her, opened the refrigerator door. As the door swung open I heard a muffled thump followed by a sharp cry of pain from Laura. She began hopping around the kitchen on one foot, blinking back tears, holding her other foot between her hands.

Alice spoke out indignantly, "Satan, in Jesus' name, I rebuke you!" Then putting her arms around Laura she looked at me, eyes flashing. "That was nothing more than a dirty trick of the devil! That olive jar just seemed to jump off the shelf!" She looked down at Laura. "Are you all right, honey?"

Laura gave a brave little smile.

Gulping, I said, "Let me tell you what I was writing at that moment." And I quoted the sentence from my notes. Alice's eyes grew angrier still.

"Just who does the devil think he is? If he thinks for one moment that by resorting to such nasty little tricks he's going to stop us from doing what God has called us to do, he's badly mistaken! We'll just work for Jesus all the harder, that's what we'll do!"

A strange kind of elation rose in my chest, and I started to laugh in spite of myself. "The devil overstepped himself that time," I said. "Actually, he's paying us a backhanded kind of compliment! The ministry we're in must be hurting him; that's why these little tricks." And right there in the kitchen, Alice and Laura and I praised God aloud for the privilege of serving Him.

I must truthfully admit the harassments still appear from time to time, even to this day, but we simply recognize them as confirmation that we are going in the right direction.

7. *I had to learn the hard way how to face deliverance attempts that failed.*

For there are failures. In fact, some whom the Lord seems deliberately to have placed in my path in order to receive help, still fail to receive or to keep it. Like Carol Stewart . . .

One day after a convention in Atlanta, I caught a cab to the airport. I was on my way to Cleveland with a flight change at Pittsburgh. But the cab became hopelessly snarled in morning rush-hour traffic and by the time we reached the terminal the plane to Pittsburgh had left. Luckily, within the hour I secured a seat on another flight, this one via New York. The last passenger to board was a woman wearing a broad-brimmed hat and dark glasses. She hesitated in the aisle.

"Is this seat taken?" she motioned to the vacant seat beside me. I smiled and shook my head.

The woman lowered herself into the seat with some difficulty, obviously in pain. Up close I could see that carefully applied makeup was covering a mass of bruises. Her lower lip was cut and swollen and even through the sunglasses I could tell that one eye was puffed half shut.

"I suppose you're going to ask if I was in an accident," the woman said. I turned away in embarrassment, realizing I had been staring. "It was no accident," she went on. "He did it on purpose."

So of course I turned back to her again. I told the woman I was a minister and asked if she would like to talk about what had happened. She sighed and leaned back against the seat. For forty-five minutes Carol Stewart told me her story. She had fallen in love with her employer, a married man. Divorce followed. She and her boss were then married and had flown to Mexico on their wedding trip.

"He got drunk on our wedding night," she said. And then with surprising frankness she told me that she discovered she had married a sadist. "When I told him I couldn't take it anymore, he sent me packing. I'm going to New York to see a doctor, then I'll file for divorce. You're a minister. Do you think God is punishing me?"

I chose my words carefully. "I think God understands all about the mess you're in, and I think He wants to help you. You made a mistake and are suffering for it, but I believe God is on your side. Perhaps He worked it out for me to miss an earlier flight this morning just so I could tell you of Jesus' love for you and how much He wants to help."

"Well, I don't know anyone who needs it more." And in a strangely appealing gesture she clasped her hands together in her lap and bowed her head. I prayed a brief prayer, simply asking God to work a miracle in her life. As I finished the wheels of the plane touched the runway.

"I change planes here," I said. Taking a card from my wallet I told her, "In two weeks I'm going to be back here in New York." I wrote the name and address of the church on the back of the card. "I'd like to have you come to the service."

I doubted that I would ever see her again, but I was wrong.

Two weeks later in the New York church I saw her sitting right up near the front. My message that night was on deliverance. After the meeting a few people remained for ministry, including Carol Stewart.

"Do you remember me?" she said. "We met on the plane."

"Of course."

"Let me ask you. I've had such a strong urge to take my life since . . . well . . . Do you think that could be caused by an evil spirit?"

"It could," I said. We quickly identified the spirits of depression and suicide and I commanded the demons to leave. It seemed to me as she got up from her knees that I could actually see the difference in her.

"Do you think something really happened? Do you think I'll be all right now?"

"I think you will," I said. "But you must keep on trusting God that you really are free."

I would have liked to talk more. But meetings never seem to allow enough time. Someone interrupted and I had no further opportunity to speak with Carol.

One week from that night I received a letter from the pastor of the church where I had ministered in New York. It contained a terse, sympathetic note folded around a newspaper clipping.

Dear Don,
Since you ministered to this young lady I thought you would want to see the enclosed clipping. Sorry things didn't work out better.

I could scarcely force myself to read the brief news account describing the death of Carol Stewart. In its usual circumspect way the paper indicated that she was the victim of an overdose of barbiturates.

Feeling sick at my stomach I let the clipping slip from my

fingers. Waves of guilt washed over me. I leaned forward across
my desk and rested my head on my arms, praying earnestly
that God forgive me. But though I knew with my mind that
forgiveness was mine, for many weeks I dragged about under a
crushing sense of failure.

Actually it was the continuing experiences with deliverance
which helped the most. Following Carol's death other people who
came for help received it abundantly; the dramatic change in
some of them could not be denied. I gradually came to realize
that in spiritual warfare, as in any kind of war, one side never wins
all the battles. The final victory is Christ's; till then I must expect
my share of defeats.

By the time I had compiled the record of mistakes and put it
in a letter to the Combeses a strange nagging anxiety had settled
in the pit of my stomach. It's all this raking over failures and
errors, I told myself: I've just worked up a good case of the
blues. Now that it's done, I'll start to feel better . . . .

15

An Afternoon at the Movies

As THE days passed the feeling persisted, a kind of vague apprehension that seemed to follow me like a shadow, everywhere I ministered. Then, as I was returning from a weekend seminar in Virginia, I found myself face to face with a half-forgotten enemy.

The weather was cold and wet as I boarded the plane at Richmond. Immediately after takeoff we were swallowed up in overcast. Unaccountably, my heart began to pound. I felt the same rising sense of dread I had experienced that day so long ago, walking into the hospital in Sharon. The fear was so real I could almost taste it. "You'll never make it home," something inside me wailed. "The plane is going to crash!"

Normally I have no fear of flying, in fact I thoroughly enjoy it. As a licensed private pilot I have endured my share of tense moments without panic. Once the small aircraft I was piloting cut out far from an airstrip and I was forced to make an emergency landing in a field of waist-high wheat. Neither my passenger, I, nor the plane was hurt and I stayed calm throughout the episode.

Yet now in this large instrument-aided airliner, an insane fear of crashing turned my arms and legs to jelly. I peered out the window at a wall of gray fog. I couldn't even see the wingtip.

"Are we climbing or diving?" I wondered crazily. "We could be stalling right now." I tried to grip the arm rests but my hands were so weak I could scarcely close them. Then I tried to will the aircraft into a normal attitude by staring straight down the cabin aisle, but it didn't help. I felt certain we were in a steep climbing turn and that any minute we would nose over and plunge to the earth.

I shut my eyes and began to pray. A scripture verse popped into my mind: "Resist Satan and he will flee from you." Summoning my courage I began to say repeatedly under my breath, "Satan, in the name of Jesus, leave me alone." After repeating the prayer more than a dozen times I found myself breathing a little easier. Slowly I opened my eyes and looked around. Across the aisle a businessman was reading his newspaper. A stewardess strolled past with a stack of magazines. Seeing the whole cabin normal and peaceful I felt the fear begin to recede, crawling back into its hiding place. By the time the plane landed at Ft. Lauderdale I was feeling fairly normal again, except for a dull ache at the base of my spine.

Alice met me at the gate. "Are you feeling all right, Don?"

"It was a rough flight," I answered evasively.

Yet it was not the flight, I knew that. The apprehension which had dogged me built during the evening until I began to feel physically ill. The fear and dread I had felt on the plane belonged to something I thought I had left safely behind me in Sharon and I was deeply dismayed by its reappearance.

The next morning was no better. The ache in my back, in fact, was worse. Every time the telephone rang my heart would jump and every little noise irritated me.

I was alone in the house most of the day with the children in school and Alice shopping, trying to work at my desk. Normally I would have welcomed the peace and quiet, but that day I couldn't concentrate. I felt as if some evil specter were standing right behind me. The sense of foreboding was almost unbearable.

The weather didn't help. It was a muggy, gray day with a restless wind whipping the trees. The very atmosphere seemed hostile. By noon the pain in my back made it impossible to sit at my desk any longer.

"I've got to get out of this spooky house," I told myself. Climbing into the car I backed out the driveway. There was a blast of horn and a screeching of tires. I jammed on my brakes and twisted my head just in time to catch a glimpse of a panel truck with its white-faced driver swerving on two wheels up onto my neighbor's yard. He managed to miss me by inches. The truck roared off while the driver's companion mouthed some words I was glad I couldn't hear.

Too unnerved to drive far, I stopped at the closest restaurant and ordered some food, which I picked at miserably. Half an hour later I drove home and entered the silent house. I stretched out on the living room couch and fell into a fitful sleep only to have a nightmare in which I relived the near accident. I woke up in a cold sweat, my heart pounding.

"If this keeps up," I thought, "I'll be a candidate for the asylum by the end of the week."

I was both relieved and irritated when Alice and the kids got home. I thought my sense of foreboding would ease with the family around me, but it didn't. After I had snapped at the kids for the second time, Alice said: "Have a hard day?"

I nodded. "I feel miserable. And when I went out to lunch I nearly got hit by a truck." I didn't bother telling her it was my fault.

"Maybe you're coming down with something." She put her cool hand on my forehead. "Why don't you stay in bed tomorrow?"

The following morning nothing had changed, so I took Alice's advice and stayed in bed. But despite the nerves and the backache I knew I was not physically ill. It was something else. I wrestled against my depression most of the morning, trying to read my Bible, trying to pray.

Alice brought me lunch on a tray. "Feeling any better?" she asked.

"Not really, but it's nice to be pampered."

"Will you be all right if I leave for a while?" There was love and concern in her voice.

"Of course. I've got a tape I want to listen to, anyhow."

So Alice left. The house was ominously quiet and just as unfriendly as the day before. Determined not to let this one go to waste too, I set the tape recorder beside the bed and put on a tape by Derek Prince on which I had wanted to make notes. How could it be that having heard the tape several times before, today for the first time I really *heard* what he was saying?

> We've found that evil spirits may gain entrance into a personality through one of many ways. The cause may be the deliberate and repeated indulgence of some appetite of the flesh. Or an unexpected tragedy or grief may make one vulnerable. In short, any kind of strain or shock which causes what we might call a breach in the person's normal defenses offers evil spirits an opportunity.
>
> Take fear, for instance. [At the word *fear* something inside me constricted.] A mother places her small child in front of the television to watch a children's program while she goes to another part of the house to work. Unknown to her, the program ends and a horror movie comes on. The child sits before the television and becomes terrified and a spirit of fear rides in.

My heart began to pound furiously against my ribs as I listened to the recorded words. I somehow sensed that what Derek was saying had great significance for me personally. I also had the distinct feeling of something inside trying to smother memory, blocking out some particular experience which was related to what Derek had said. I closed my eyes and tried to concentrate. It was something way back in my life—back even before my teens.

Then all at once I remembered. The incident swept with cruel clarity into my mind.

I had been only eight or nine at the time. It was a hot summer day. My brother Hal and I caught the bus to town to go to the movies. But instead of seeing the western film Mother had given us permission to see, Hal dragged me to another theater. He had already paid our admission and led me inside before I discovered it was a horror show, one of the classic vampire films of the thirties. The eerie music, the haunted house, the stormy night, the moans and the ghostly screams. Worst of all, the vampire— that satanic leering face, half hidden behind the black cape . . . .

I was petrified with fear and pleaded with my brother to leave. "Hal, let's go home, I'm scared!"

But Hal was four years older than I and those four years had placed him safely beyond the terror that was reaching for me. "Be quiet. It's only a movie. Nothing can really happen."

"But I'm scared. I want to go home."

"If you're such a big fraidy-cat, wait for me outside!"

But I was far too terrified to head up the long dark aisle alone. That horrible blood-sucking thing might grab me before I could reach the safety of sunlight. Yet to stay was torture too, beyond anything I had ever endured. I squeezed my eyes tight against the horror on the screen, but I could not block out the sound. I buried my face against the sweaty, smelly back of the seat and cringed and cowered and shook until—recalling those desperate moments I am convinced—I became possessed by fear.

Terror hidden for thirty-five years began to emerge as I sat there on my bed listening to the even voice on the tape machine. All at once the dread enemy inside rushed out of hiding, screaming against the walls of my mind.

Fear! Fear!

The thing was naming itself. Only this time it was not the same as when it had attacked me in the hospital and in the airplane. For despite my violent trembling and churning stomach and the piercing pain in my back, this time I somehow felt as if the spotlight of God's love had been turned on inside me, forcing the frightening, crawly thing within to reveal itself. It wasn't me screaming, this time. It was the thing itself, the arch enemy of my life confessing its name.

Fear that had caused me so much misery. Fear, the enemy of peace and the opponent of trust. Fear of failure, fear of rejection, fear of poverty, fear of living, fear of dying. Fear, fear, fear!

And before I could renounce it or command it to come out, it began to move.

First I felt something like roots tear loose from the lower part of my back, right in those vertebrae where the throb and ache were located. Then the thing moved into my midriff, rolling and churning and convulsing. I felt it rising up through my chest and into my throat, choking me. I doubled over the side of the bed and began to retch in an ugly gasping convulsion.

Yet somehow, even then, I could feel the presence of God. It was as if I were some kind of sponge filled with dirty water being twisted and wrung out by a pair of giant loving hands. I retched one more time and a stream of hot bile came out of my nose and mouth, and I could sense I was in physical contact with the true nature of the filthy spirit which had lodged within me.

Then as suddenly as they had begun, the gagging and the convulsion ceased.

Cautiously I raised up, and— Oh! I cannot describe what I felt like. It was as if I had experienced some kind of inner bath or shower. I felt shining clean and at peace—a peace such as I had never known. The whole room seemed filled with the presence of Jesus, as though He had been standing, all my life, with arms stretched out to me in Love. Delivered . . . . Until that moment I had always believed it was: delivered *from*. But, oh how much more it is: delivered *into* that immense compassion.

"Jesus!" I heard myself crying, "Lord Jesus, thank you!"

With tears of gratitude still spilling out of my eyes, I once again became aware of the tape recorder. It was still running. Derek's steady voice was quoting the familiar verse from Joel:

> And it shall come to pass that all who call upon the name of the Lord shall be delivered.

Later, of course, there were questions.

Why had I not recognized the source of my torment before? Why had my own fear remained entrenched when I came (successfully) against the same spirit in others? Why, after so many years of struggle, had I been unable to see, or to admit, that the source of this problem was an evil spirit? Had it been pride? Or perhaps fear itself which kept me from admitting to a spirit of fear?

I'm still working on these questions. But now I know that I do not have to have the answers before I can have the freedom. There is much, much still to learn about evil spirits and exorcism. But God does not require of us intellectual understanding before He will give us the fulfillment of His promises. Like millions of others, I had been a victim. Like a growing host I was now free, with only the responsibility ahead of me of staying close to my Deliverer.

16

The Deliverance Ministry Grows

FREE from a major bondage in my own life, I could minister with a confidence I had never known before. While the deliverance ministry remained difficult and some who came to me I could not seem to help, nevertheless there was a much higher proportion of success than before. As I continued to travel back and forth across the country I learned more about the amazing work God had called me into. For example, I began to see additional gifts of the Holy Spirit emerge in my ministry. I had already, with Max's deliverance, experienced the word of Knowledge. Now I also began to experience the gift of Discerning of spirits.

One night I paid a return visit to the church in central Florida where Joe Wheeler had been delivered of the spirit of confusion. After the service the minister and I stood at the door shaking hands with people as they walked past. One woman lingered behind. With a sinking feeling I recognized that stringy blonde hair. It was Sister Sadie. I braced myself for a tirade, but to my surprise, when Sadie stepped up at last, her voice was almost timid.

"Mr. Basham, I know you must not think very kindly of me

after the things I said when you were here before. But—can you stay long enough to pray for me?"

The change in Sadie was astonishing. In the pastor's office she went on: "I've been very upset lately. I can't sleep. I want to be delivered."

"Delivered from what?" I asked gently.

"Well . . ." Sadie hesitated. "I—I want to be delivered from whatever it is that . . ." She paused again, wringing her hands. Then a mirthless smile creased her face, a note of arrogance stole into her voice.

"I want to be delivered from whatever it is that keeps me from telling people about the wonderful dreams and visions God has given me!"

I felt sure the demonic thing tormenting her was beginning to surface. "What kind of dreams and visions, Sadie?" I asked warily.

Sadie closed her eyes and began rocking back and forth on the chair. Her voice took on an eerie crooning sound.

"Oh, all the glorious dreams and visions! All of them! There's one in particular. I'm walking through this street of fire and I see this handsome, princely figure. He tells me He's the Lord but there's this terrible black veil over His face. He tells me not to be frightened—"

The wailing voice went on but I had heard enough. Recalling the advice in the first epistle of John about testing the spirits, I said, "Spirit, I command you to answer me; will you confess that Jesus Christ has come in the flesh?"

At my words Sadie's lips clamped shut. I repeated the command but Sadie remained silent. After a few seconds she stood up and in the same crooning voice resumed her chant. "Oh, the beautiful dreams and visions which I must share with the world . . . ."

All at once I *knew* the name of the spirit. It was a "spirit of false prophecy." Grateful for the sudden insight I gave a stern command.

"You spirit of false prophecy, I command you in the name of Jesus Christ to come out of her."

The results were immediate. Sadie let out a loud shriek and dropped to her knees as the demon came out. Bending over her I could see tears streaming down her cheeks and hear her whispering her thanks to Jesus.

We talked for a while more in the pastor's office, he and I marveling at the transformation in the woman before us. Gone was the harshness, the tendency to find fault—and all talk of a black-veiled Jesus!

Later, after Sadie had left, the pastor said, "Don, how did you know that it was a spirit of false prophecy?"

"The Lord just suddenly showed me. Clear as though I'd heard the words." From that night on, at frequent intervals, I have experienced again this strange but wonderful gift, as an aid in the deliverance ministry.

Naturally, I was grateful for this additional operation of the Holy Spirit. But increased effectiveness in ministry brought increased problems. The mounting number of people clamoring for help became an almost unbearable frustration. Every time I spoke on the subject of deliverance I ended up counseling and praying with people for hours afterward. Even then there was never enough time, and many troubled people would grow tired of waiting and leave.

"But what more can I do?" I wondered. On top of the grinding hours of ministry, life at home began to suffer. There were telephone calls at all hours of the day and night.

"Reverend Basham, I hate to call you in the middle of the night like this, but I'm desperate. . . . When will you be speaking in Pittsburgh?" Or Dallas. Or New Orleans. Or Los Angeles.

Often the person calling would offer to drive or fly to Florida to see me personally, a suggestion I continually discouraged.

Others didn't wait to telephone, they just came. Sometimes the first inkling would be a telephone call from the edge of town. "Reverend Basham, I'm at the Pompano exit of the Florida Turnpike. Can you give me directions to your house?" Other times they just appeared at the door. I began to dread seeing a car turn in the driveway.

There was constant tension between attempting to preserve some privacy for our family and trying to help those who really needed it. I tried not to be critical of the people who imposed themselves upon us. Caught up in their own pressing troubles, their need often blinded them to the rights of others.

Still, the problem seemed overwhelming. As one man with a very limited ministry, how could I even make a dent in such a mountain of human need? Then something happened which promised at least a partial solution.

Alice and I were trying to spend a quiet evening at home when, as on many another evening, we were interrupted. A family seeking deliverance for their thirteen-year-old daughter. A spirit of asthma identified itself and spoke through the girl's own lips.

"I won't come out," it snarled. "This girl belongs to me!" Then, as I commanded the spirit to leave, the girl's eleven-year-old brother who had been sitting across the room suddenly began to gasp. "No! No!" a whiny voice spoke out of him. "I won't come out either!"

I turned to the parents, astonished. Yes, they said, the boy, too, had had a lifelong history of breathing problems, though not so severe as his sister's. At length both children went through the typical contortions of an asthmatic attack, followed by sudden happy relief. *Identical spirits of asthma left sister and brother simultaneously!* As the significance of what I had seen began to sink in, my heart began to thump. If two people could be delivered by a single command, why not ten? Twenty?

I didn't sleep much that night as I pondered and prayed over such a bold possibility. Could God merely have been waiting until I was freed from fear before showing me this greater authority in the name of Jesus? Hadn't I been praying for a way to help more people? Could group deliverance be God's answer to that prayer? To find out I would have to try and see.

The opportunity came a few weeks later. I had been in New England for several days and was scheduled for one final service before flying home. The minister who had arranged my itinerary was driving me to the town where the final meeting was to be held.

"You will be speaking in an interdenominational church tonight, Don," John Travis told me. "The congregation has a new minister who's been with them only about six months. We're having dinner with him and his wife beforehand."

A few minutes later we pulled up before a neat Cape Cod cottage next door to a large stone church. The front door swung open as I climbed out of the car.

"Come in, come in!" Surely I knew that deep resonant voice? I glanced toward the house. To my amazement the man shaking hands with John Travis was Dr. Willard Thompson, the minister who two years before had made such mincemeat of me in that ministers' meeting in Washington.

"Don't just stand there, Don," he laughed. "I know how surprised you must be, but you really are in the right place."

John Travis looked puzzled. "You two know each other?"

"After a fashion," Dr. Thompson replied. "Come in and I'll explain. But first I want you to meet my wife. She's the one who's really responsible for all this."

A short plump woman with the merriest eyes I have ever seen

reached for my hand. "I'm Amelia," she said. "And I've been looking forward to meeting you ever since my husband came home from that ministers' lunch complaining about you."

"You see, John, at that time I didn't believe God was still in the miracle-working business," Dr. Thompson explained. He shook his head remembering. "But a lot has happened since that meeting. It all started with Amelia's healing."

We listened in amazement as Dr. Thompson told us that the energetic lady before us had been bedfast with a heart ailment for over three years. But not long after that same ministers' meeting, some women from Dr. Thompson's own church came to pray for their pastor's wife. She was healed forthwith. Unable to deny what he saw with his eyes, Dr. Thompson began to read and study Scriptures concerning such things and ended with a completely reversed theology. "In one week I changed from a skeptic to an ardent believer," Dr. Thompson continued. "Of course, having a living miracle to cook breakfast for me every morning helped the transition."

But when Dr. Thompson began to proclaim his new beliefs from the pulpit, there was an immediate reaction. Almost before he knew what had happened there was a special meeting of his church board where it was voted that Dr. Thompson should immediately be "retired."

"So when we received the invitation to come to this church, we accepted," Dr. Thompson said. "We've been here six months now and we're happier than we've been in years. I've been telling my people about your ministry of deliverance, Don, so feel free to conduct tonight's meeting in any way you choose. I trust you."

Was this the invitation to try a group deliverance service?

The final hour before the meeting I spent in Dr. Thompson's study praying, and as I entered the pulpit I felt as ready as I ever would. For an hour I spoke on deliverance, giving basic scriptural background and illustrating with my own experience. I concluded the message with an invitation.

"I believe some of you can be helped by this ministry. I urge you to be honest with yourself and with God. If you feel you are in some form of bondage, then it is quite possible that the cause may be an evil spirit. This will not be a ministry open to the idly curious, but if you are sincere in your desire to be set free, please stay."

Dr. Thompson suggested we use one of the Sunday school rooms in the church basement for ministry. Nearly fifty people trooped down the stairs after me. One woman gave me a tremulous smile as she entered the schoolroom.

"I felt positively terrified of coming to this service," she confessed, "and I couldn't imagine why. Now I know I need to be delivered and whatever it is didn't want me to come!"

After everyone had found a seat, I began.

"There are too many of you for me to pray with each one individually. But this is not necessary." (At least I fervently hoped it was not.) "You can assist in your own deliverance."

To set the stage I led them through two prayers of preparation: a prayer of renunciation of all psychic practice, and a prayer of forgiveness for every person who had in any way injured them. I listened as people all over the room began quietly to speak out the names of those they needed to forgive: father, mother, husband, wife, brother, teacher, employer, pastor, neighbor, self. Some began to weep openly as they gave up resentments and hatreds they had carried for years.

Last of all I led them through a simple prayer in which they reaffirmed their faith in the Lord Jesus Christ, claiming once more His sacrifice on the Cross as the basis for their salvation and deliverance. Then I glanced around the room.

"Now I intend to take authority over every evil spirit tormenting anyone in this room. If you feel something rising up within you, renounce it in the name of Jesus and expel it. You might even try breathing out sharply, or even coughing. Some of you may feel like weeping or letting out a little cry. Don't let that embarrass you. Whatever it is that's inside you, you want it out."

I paused and under my breath prayed, "Lord, help me! *You* are the Deliverer." Then I spoke aloud.

"In the name of Jesus Christ I come against every evil spirit tormenting the people in this room. I command you to loose your hold and to come out! Every spirit of bondage and torment, every spirit of sickness and infirmity, every unclean sex spirit, I command you all to reveal yourselves and to come out!"

For almost a half-minute nothing whatever happened. Perhaps, after all, it was not possible to . . . and then, all over the room, a chorus of low moans and sighs began to swell. A slender gray-haired man directly in front of me began to tremble. I bent over him and commanded the spirit to identify itself. He grabbed me by the shoulders with both hands. "N-n-nerves!" And in the same breath the spirit fled.

Near the end of the front row a teen-aged boy was clenching and unclenching his fists. "I hate him!" he said. "I hate him!" I placed a hand on his head. "You can get rid of that spirit of hate, son," I said. "Would you like that?" The boy nodded.

Then a sudden inspiration hit me. To those sitting near I said, "Everyone troubled right now by hatred, repeat after me: "In the name of Jesus, I renounce hatred!" At least a dozen people repeated the prayer. When I gave the command for these spirits to leave, a volley of coughs erupted. Something *was* happening! Silently I thanked God for my own deliverance from fear, knowing full well that without it, I would never have had the courage to minister in such a bold manner.

As the deliverance continued the power of God became increasingly apparent in that basement room. Although outwardly there seemed little structure to what was happening, there was a kind of relentless divine initiative discernible, as if an invisible army of angels were at work.

To my surprise, some who received deliverance turned and at once began helping others. One young man glanced up at me. "Like it says, 'Freely ye have received, freely give.' "

Moments later, Willard Thompson came over, his face tear-stained but smiling. "John Travis just prayed for me and I was delivered from the demon of pride," he said. "I feel twenty years younger! For years the thing's been like a steel spring coiled up inside me."

The ministry continued for almost an hour until it seemed almost everyone present had received a measure of help, and my heart was filled with gratitude at what I had seen the Lord accomplish. To dismiss the people, Dr. Thompson led them in a hymn of thanksgiving. As the rising crescendo of praise filled the room, I felt we were reaching the very throne of grace. The presence of Jesus was so strong the air itself seemed to pulse with glory. It was a majestic, awesome moment; one I shall never forget.

But to my dismay, group deliverance did not lighten my load as I had hoped; instead it intensified it. The very nature of such sessions automatically included the new Christian as well as the experienced one, the unbalanced along with the mentally stable, the emotionally dependent together with the mature, with no chance to sort out these varying degrees of preparedness or counsel individually. I might have expected trouble—and it came.

About three months after the service in Dr. Thompson's church, I ministered group deliverance, as I was doing increasingly often, in a certain southern city at the invitation of a group of local clergy. At the time the ministry seemed highly successful with a number of people receiving dramatic deliverance. Two weeks later came the phone call. . . .

It was the pastor of one of the sponsoring churches. A woman in his congregation—an insecure individual whom he had been counseling for many weeks—had attended the deliverance service. Initially she had seemed much improved. Anxieties which had troubled her for years disappeared, and with great enthusiasm she began testifying to her deliverance. Then, however, she had attempted to bring the same results to others. Two days before this phone call she had undertaken to minister to a whole roomful of people at a house prayer meeting. One person had suffered a violent physical manifestation, screaming and falling on the floor, terrifying everyone. The self-styled leader had broken down and begun to weep. The meeting ended in fear and confusion, and the woman had retreated into all her former problems. Naturally the pastor blamed me.

"That's the trouble with this buckshot deliverance of yours, Basham," his voice crackled angrily over the telephone. "You don't know who's going to be there and you can do a lot of damage. My people are totally confused and divided—and talking about nothing but demons."

I hung up the phone more despondent than I had felt in many months. As so often before in this baffling ministry, I heartily wished I had never got involved. I couldn't see myself down the years continuing a ministry which created nothing but uproar, controversy, and division. Bit by bit I would extricate myself, return to mentioning deliverance only on rare occasions, minister it only privately and with carefully selected persons. . . .

But even as I contemplated such a retreat, God began dealing with me. He reminded me that this was His ministry, and that He had not put me through years of training and experience in it to cut and run from the problems that seemed invariably to follow each breakthrough. He showed me that the problem I was facing now resulted not from the deliverance ministry itself, but from *abuse* of the ministry, and that there were things that I could do to head off such abuse. He began to show me that other aspects of the spiritual renewal appearing in the church today could be brought to bear on this problem.

One was the principle of the authority of local spiritual leadership. In practically every town or city where I ministered, I was becoming aware of the emergence of a committed body of "elders" —dynamic Spirit-led Christians, both clergy and lay, who accepted responsibility for the spiritual well-being of their communities.

I came to see that I should never try and minister deliverance without the active involvement of these elders who would then *be prepared to shepherd and nurture the people* in whatever blessings they received from outside ministry—whether healing, deliverance, spiritual gifts, or any other benefit. After I had shared with a given group what I had been invited to share, the major responsibility for follow through would lie with these spiritual overseers.

In addition, I saw the necessity for applying the scriptural principle of selective ministries. Paul reminds us that not everyone is called to the same service: "And God hath set some in the church, first apostles, secondarily prophets, thirdly teachers, after that miracles, then gifts of healings . . . ." Obviously, not everyone benefiting from deliverance was going to be set in a ministry of deliverance, any more than everyone who receives healing through prayer will automatically have a ministry of healing. The woman who had tried to assume authority for deliverance and failed was a case in point. At that point she had needed guidance and encouragement in keeping her own deliverance, not the burden of ministering to others.

So I came to see that there were three essential factors involved in the presentation of group deliverance. (*1*) Recognition of the need for this ministry by the recognized spiritual leadership in a given area *before the invitation to an "outside authority" goes out*. (*2*) Clear scriptural teaching on the ministry followed by demonstration. (*3*) Careful follow-up by local leaders, setting deliverance into the total spiritual ministry available to Christians in that place.

I was grateful for this increased vision, and grateful to the minister whose irate phone call had brought it about. But I was back face-to-face with my old enemy, too little time! Apparently group deliverance was not going to reduce the demands on me, but increase them. Ahead of me loomed longer hours, longer stints away from home, pre-meeting meetings with clergy and lay leaders, post-meeting meetings with those who would stand by for possible dislocations and repercussions—a never-ending spiral of responsibility.

Then God very lovingly began to show me that He never intended me to be "our-man-in-charge-of-deliverance." Rather, it was a ministry which He was restoring to the whole Body of Christ. To my surprise and relief, I began to hear good news from some of the cities where I had ministered. Some who had been set free had indeed been called to minister to others. I heard from ministers, missionaries, medical doctors, businessmen, all beginning to assert with authority the mighty name of Jesus Christ.

One of the first letters came from Stella Sweeney, who had received such a spectacular deliverance at Jack and Anne Musselman's home. Stella had returned to New England where all kinds of opportunity to witness had begun to open to her, and she had found herself not only testifying to her own deliverance but praying effectively for the release of others as well.

And there were additional letters from Ray and Lucy Coombes in Atlanta, Georgia, as they continued to minister with great power. Ray's experience as a medical doctor helped. Where lesser-trained men might have held back for fear of trespassing on a doctor's territory, Ray could add medical insight to the spiritual.

The same thing proved true with Dr. Ed Atkinson of Greenville, Pennsylvania, and Dr. Lawton Smith of Miami, Florida. All three of these men of medicine found themselves, as Spirit-baptized

Christians, adding the dimension of deliverance to their vocation of healing.

I witnessed the development of another ministry of deliverance in a former missionary to Africa, Mrs. Pat Brooks of Ballston Lake, New York. Pat, who herself had been delivered from demonic torment which had forced a premature retirement from the mission field, had already begun to teach and minister deliverance before I met her. After attending a seminar near Albany, New York, where I presented the group deliverance ministry, she immediately began to minister in similar fashion. An effective writer as well, Pat has written—from sad personal experience—a number of magazine articles on the danger of occultism.

Soon I had amassed quite a list of names of Christians being effectively used in deliverance.* And as I did, of course, I discovered that while God had led me to employ certain techniques, others used other means. One was the practice of praying "in the Spirit" or tongues. The deliverance of a doctor friend was a case in point.

Dr. Lawton Smith, a medical doctor in Miami, on hearing of this ministry sought help for himself from a Christian group in that area. Many spirits were cast out and Lawton Smith's personal testimony to his deliverance is a thrilling one. Significantly, during a difficult time in the deliverance, one of the men ministering was suddenly led to begin praying loudly in tongues. Immediately a demon manifested itself in Lawton, twisting his face grotesquely.

"Stop it!" the demon cried. "Don't pray that way! That's a perfect prayer! A perfect prayer! We can't stand it!" And with that the demon came out. Paul describes how this form of prayer works in Romans 8: "Likewise the Spirit also helpeth our infirmities: for we know not what we should pray for as we ought: but the Spirit itself maketh intercession for us . . . ."

* A list of deliverance ministries in various parts of the country is provided in Appendix B (pp. 223–224).

Then a strange experience in Georgia taught me how at times simply a period of praise in which we exalt Jesus can put demons to flight. The incident occurred as some friends and I were praying for people to receive the baptism in the Holy Spirit. We were ministering to about twenty people simultaneously, and some were already entering into the joyous experience, when one woman began to laugh, not for joy, but in a kind of harsh, sarcastic way. As I approached the chair where she was sitting I saw her face frozen in a sneer. Recognizing it as some demon spirit which had surfaced in reaction to our prayers—although nothing whatever had been said about demons—I commanded it to be silent and to come out. But the demon simply laughed harder than ever.

I took the woman by the shoulders and told her to stop laughing, but apparently she was helpless in the spirit's grasp. She made gestures with her hands and shook her head, but could not stop the wild laughter.

"Can you hear what I'm saying?" I asked her. She nodded her head. "Then exercise your will against that tormentor," I advised. "And in Jesus' name I command that spirit to be silent!" She shook her head helplessly as the laughter continued. There was real terror in her eyes.

My friends had grouped themselves supportively around us. "Don," one of them suggested, "let's just praise Jesus."

We joined hands in a circle around the distressed lady and plunged into the familiar chorus,

> There is power, power, wonderworking power,
> In the blood of the Lamb,
> There is power, power, wonderworking power
> In the precious blood of the Lamb.

Over and over again we sang it as the laughter became shriller and shriller. Finally, after about the sixth time, the woman lunged to her feet and with a cry the demon came out.

Collapsing back on her chair she gasped, "It's stopped! Whatever it was—it couldn't stand to hear about the blood of Jesus. I could hear it inside me saying, 'No! No! No!' "

On several occasions since that time, when the demons seem to be putting up more resistance than usual, I have felt prompted to have an entire congregation sing hymns magnifying the beauty and wholeness of Jesus in the face of the ugliness confronting us. An immediate increase in effective deliverance always seems to follow.

But even as my experience in these matters grew, and even as I saw other Christians grasp the sword of deliverance and wield it with effectiveness, there were two persistent problems, both of which seemed only intensified by the spread of the ministry.

Problem No. 1: How could proper teaching about deliverance precede or even catch up with the wild rumors and fears which seemed to outdistance the ministry itself? *Problem No. 2:* How could I continue to work in this important area without giving credence to the charge of having a lopsided ministry, of being a "demon-chaser"?

Both problems, I knew, stemmed in part from the shock element of such a subject in the twentieth century. When a topic that has been the province of cartoonists and fantasy writers is suddenly put forward seriously, distortions are going to follow. In one midwestern city I gave a series of six Bible studies, only one of which dealt with the deliverance ministry. The newspapers ignored five of the talks but gleefully played up the sixth: "Preacher Warns Faithful to Beware of Little Red Devils."

If I let fear of being misrepresented influence me to the point of keeping silent about deliverance during a particular seminar, then, of course, there were no lurid headlines. But my silence also meant that people needing deliverance would not receive it.

On the other hand, to teach and demonstrate deliverance inevitably made waves after I left the community. Some of the opposition was due to the very real ugliness of certain moments during this ministry. Many, perhaps most, deliverances are quiet and unfrightening. But, of course, in any public service it is the noisy and acrobatic ones that get noticed, and—as I attempt to forewarn people—we have an ugly enemy. I searched the Bible again and again for any evidence that Jesus took people into a corner or behind a closed door before delivering them, to spare onlookers an uncouth spectacle. His deliverances all seem to have been accomplished in public, in full view of crowds of people.

But there persists, especially in church circles, the feeling that religion should be "nice," dressed in clean shirt and white gloves. This is true, doubtless, of our times of formal worship when we come together to honor our Lord; the Sunday morning service is hardly the time to minister deliverance. On the other hand, the good news of this ministry is that when we gather in some drafty basement room to seek release for tormented people, Jesus is as sovereignly present as among the flowers and carpeted aisles upstairs. But it's not going to be a polite experience, because the devil is not polite. Jesus, when He walked the earth, did not shrink from starkest ugliness; in our day we have grown fastidious.

It created a baffling and frustrating dilemma. Years earlier I had resigned myself to the opposition of good Christian people who rejected the baptism and gifts of the Holy Spirit; who labeled the charismatic movement in the Church as "emotionalism" or "fanaticism." Now I saw the same spirit of accusation coming from people who were baptized in the Holy Spirit but drew the line at deliverance. One well-known Bible teacher, whom I greatly respect and admire, collared me at a charismatic seminar one day to give me some fatherly advice.

"Don, you've had a fine ministry and you've written a fine book about the power of God in your life," he said. "Now you're throwing it all away over this demon business! You're creating demons in the minds of people just by talking about them!" No argument or testimony of mine could convince him that the deliverance ministry was valid.

His comment, however, pointed the way to one answer to Problem No. 1: I had written a book before, I could do so again! A book would provide opportunity as no amount of meetings ever would to present deliverance as I myself had encountered it, step by slow, reluctant step, and above all to present Christ as the all-powerful, all-compassionate Deliverer. The result is in your hands, in the prayerful hope that it can speak peace, both to those who have been too little aware of the thief in our midst, and to those who in the first shock of discovery tend to give too much attention and importance to a foe who—if Christians but knew it— was defeated once for all time on a Cross outside Jerusalem.

As for Problem No. 2: God was soon to use the very lopsidedness of my ministry to enable me to submit myself and my work to others whom God had raised up with ministries of their own, enabling me to find a place of security and effectiveness in the Body of Christ beyond any I had ever known.

17

Right Now, in Your Own Room

As GRATEFUL as I was for the effectiveness of group deliverance, I continued to be aware of its pitfalls for the ill-prepared, the excitable, the immature in Christ. Were the wonderful results in the lives of the many worth the hurt to the few who went overboard and began discovering demons behind the coffeepot? It was while I was wrestling with this question that I came upon an answer so simple—and potentially so far-reaching—that I consider it the best news of all the welcome message of deliverance. It was the realization that Christians, once they understand the principles involved, can call upon their Deliverer without the intervention of another human being at all. I had done this very thing when I was delivered first from the demon of Spiritualism, then from the spirit of fear: but somehow it had never occurred to me that this was a universal possibility. It took an elderly New England couple to point the way.

Some months after my visit to Dr. Willard Thompson's church I was back in the northeast, ministering at a church in Connecticut. I had just concluded my second lecture when a frail, white-haired man asked if he and his wife could speak to me privately.

"We were here last night when you introduced the ministry of deliverance," the old man began. "We even stayed afterward in the prayer room and saw remarkable things apparently take place. Nevertheless, we were very skeptical and wondered if there was really anything to it."

His wife interrupted, "But when we got home, I began to feel strange; a little nauseated and very irritable. In fact, I found myself feeling very angry with Henry, and that isn't like me. I went into the bathroom and looked in the mirror and saw something in my face which wasn't nice at all. So I asked Jesus to help me and—"

"And all at once I heard a regular rumpus in the bathroom," the husband broke in excitedly. "I rushed in to see what had happened and found Edna choking, like she'd swallowed a chicken bone. I tell you, Reverend Basham, if I hadn't heard you tell the things those spirits do sometimes, I guess I would have called the doctor! But I heard her say—she could scarcely talk—'You tell me your name!' And it did! It called itself 'Pride'—"

"I commanded it in Jesus' name to go straight away," Edna interrupted once more, "and it came out with a regular screech! Today, all day long, I've felt just wonderful. For years I've been a terribly proud woman, and I just know the Lord has set me free."

As the couple related their story it was like a light turning on in my mind. Why had I not seen it before? Our authority over Satan and evil spirits is the authority of the name of Jesus Christ; therefore every Christian who acknowledges Christ's atoning death on the Cross on his behalf can—if he has the courage and meets the conditions—effect his own deliverance. And do so in the privacy of his own home where no crowd psychology or "emotionalism" can intrude on the reality of the experience.

That elderly couple, physically so fragile it seemed a puff of wind could whisk them out of sight, stood before me in the joy of the Lord, testifying to having put Satan to flight by calling on the name of Jesus. What more nudging did I need?

In the weeks that followed I began encouraging people to attempt their own deliverance and in the process developed a checklist based on the steps in Chapter 12. In this case they are tailored for the individual's own use. If you have a difficulty which you believe may stem from the presence of an evil spirit, and if you truly desire deliverance, the following procedure can be totally effective. Many, many people present in meetings where these steps have been outlined have gone home and seen themselves set free.

(On the other hand, remember that your problem may have nothing to do with demon activity! I never address a large meeting without being waited upon, afterward, by a certain number of languorous or wistful souls requesting deliverance from the "demons" of tobacco, laziness, worry, envy, or what have you, when the real trouble is their own lack of self-control, trust, love, and other hard-won virtues. Before you decide you have a demon, apply the test: have you submitted your problem to sustained prayer, discipline, and obedience to what you believe God is telling you? Only when these things have *really* been tried—and failed—is it time to consider deliverance.)

For those afflicted with genuine demon torment, here is the *checklist:*

1. *Commitment to Jesus Christ*

The promises of divine help in the New Testament are to those who belong to Jesus Christ. Therefore, deliverance begins with surrender to the Deliverer. If you have not already made that surrender, do it now. Commit (or recommit) your life to Jesus Christ and make that commitment as complete and total as you know how to make it. A prayer like the following can be effective:

Dear Lord Jesus Christ,

I confess that I have sinned and as a sinner I deserve only Your judgment and not Your mercy. But I believe You died on the Cross for me and that you shed Your own blood for my sin. I hereby confess and repent of all my sins. [Be specific: name those sins known to you.] I ask You to forgive me. I accept Your sacrifice on the Cross for me. I accept You as my personal Lord and Savior and ask that You come into my heart and rule there. Thank You for forgiving me and saving me. I promise to live for You from now on. Thank You, Lord, Amen.

2. *Forgiving Others*

There is more to forgiveness than just confessing our sins. To be forgiven we must forgive others. Jesus said, "If ye forgive not men their trespasses, neither will your Father forgive your trespasses." [Matthew 6:15] The necessity of forgiving all those who have wronged or hurt you cannot be overemphasized. Time and again, I have seen deliverance blocked by an unforgiving attitude on the part of the one seeking help; just as over and over again I have seen people set free when they finally forgive. Satan and his brood are legalists. They know what their rights are. As long as a person harbors hate and resentment and unforgiveness in his heart, the evil spirits have a *right* to remain; that resentment and hatred is the "ground" they can stand on: it is *their* territory.

"But whom must I forgive?" I am sometimes asked. The answer is, you must forgive every person whose name stirs feelings of bitterness or hostility in you; every name that rankles in memory when you think of it. Most often, it is someone close to you, whom you also love the most: husband, wife, son, daughter, father, mother, friend, business partner. No matter how much he has hurt you, how wrong he is and how right you are, you still must forgive him. Remember that forgiveness is not a feeling, it is a decision. All it requires is a simple prayer, backed by a sincere act of the will. "In the name of Jesus, I forgive _____." That's all it takes. But you cannot, you must not, bypass this step if you want deliverance.

3. *Renunciation of Occultism*

Since a major port of entry for demons is involvement in various forms of occultism, and since occultism is everywhere dramatically on the increase today, I have found it essential to have every person seeking deliverance make a definite act of renunciation and dissociation from all forms of psychic and occult phenomena.

The renunciation needs to be as complete and as emphatic as you can make it. This is no parlor game we are playing; it can mean the difference between life and death, between a frustrated life and a victorious one. In confession of sin most people name things like hate, anger, lust, gluttony, and other attitudes and appetites of the flesh, but often do not realize the more subtle evil couched in such practices as astrology, fortune-telling, witchcraft, spiritualism, palm-reading, and the like. Therefore it is necessary to take a deliberate step of abandoning and turning your back forever on all such psychic practices and occult arts.

When these necessary steps have been taken, you are ready for the act of *deliverance* itself.

1. *Identify the Specific Spirit to Be Cast Out*

In most cases it seems the spirits must be dealt with one at a time. This means identifying the spirit, renouncing it, and commanding it to come out. So, if you're not sure of the identity of the spirit, or suspect you have several and don't know which one to deal with first, it helps to command the spirit to give its name. Once the command is given in the name of Jesus, the identity of the spirit will impress itself upon your consciousness; sometimes forcibly, sometimes very gently. Since spirits express themselves in terms of their torment, you may suddenly feel the physical symptoms of, say, fear or nerves or hate.

2. *Renounce the Spirit by Name*

Having pinpointed the identity of the spirit, now renounce it by the very name it gave. "In the name of Jesus, I renounce the spirit of hate!" (or whatever). If you feel your bondage is especially severe, it may help to repeat the prayer several times, for emphasis. In fact, the first few times it may require an effort of your own will just to enunciate the words.

3. *Command the Spirit to Leave in the Name of Jesus*

Having renounced the spirit, command it to come out. "You spirit of hate, I command you to come out of me in the name of Jesus!" Be stern and insistent and repeat the command until something starts to happen. Physical symptoms which indicate the beginning of deliverance include shortness of breath, nausea, or a constricting of the throat, although deliverance may occur with none of these symptoms.

4. *Expel the Spirit*

You can sometimes help yourself in the actual physical act of deliverance by expelling your breath sharply. This may induce gagging, coughing, or other oral manifestation, since in most cases the spirits seem to leave through the mouth. You may even let out a sharp cry or scream, a belch, or a prodigious yawn.

Even if something like this happens in your case, there is no need for alarm. Stay calm in your own spirit and determined to be free. Usually the gagging or coughing lasts only a matter of seconds and is followed by a sense of relief, indicating the spirit has come out. Often, on the other hand, the spirit leaves with just a gentle sigh, a sense of "lightness," or the relaxing of inner tension.

After the first spirit has been identified, renounced, and cast out, repeat the procedure. Sometimes a person seems tormented by only one spirit, often there are more. Deliverance may continue intermittently for several days or weeks. You may break free from two or three spirits on the first attempt and feel marvelously delivered. Then a few days later, additional symptoms may appear which indicate the presence of other spirits. This is a common occurrence, so there is no need for dismay or feeling that the spirits have returned. It is simply an indication of the Holy Spirit continuing His work within you. Simply recognize that from the moment of your first deliverance the enemy is being put to rout and that it is the will and intent of the Lord Jesus Christ to set you completely free.

Postlude: Members One of Another

IT WAS 2:00 A.M. and the four of us were sitting in a hotel room in Fort Lauderdale: Charles Simpson, Bob Mumford, Derek Prince, and I. We were the teachers for a week-long Bible conference then in progress at the hotel.

Charles was the Southern Baptist minister whose brotherly word of warning had earlier rescued me from overemphasis on deliverance as the answer-to-every-need. His Bayview Heights Church in Mobile, Alabama, had long ago experienced the outpouring of the Holy Spirit. During the years of its charismatic experience the church had developed strong local elders to shepherd the congregation, freeing Charles for an increasing nationwide vocation of teaching.

Bob Mumford I had met in a seminar just six months previously. Converted to Christ while a medic in the navy, Bob had entered medical school after his discharge. Later yielding to a call to the ministry, he had graduated from a Pentecostal Bible college and attended an Episcopal seminary. Pastoring briefly before joining the faculty of a Christian college, Bob felt an increasing desire to become a Bible teacher to the church at large. Just weeks previously he had moved his home and office from California to Fort Lauderdale.

Derek and I, since our first meeting over his teapot, had become close personal friends.

Our meeting in the hotel at such an hour stemmed from our love and concern for a fellow minister in trouble; a fine man who under great stress had fallen prey to a particularly tragic form of immorality. But even as we prayed for our friend, God began dealing with the four of us. Charles Simpson was the first to glimpse what was happening.

"You know, it's not just for Frank's sake the four of us are here. Not one of us is immune from the deception which trapped Frank. His difficulty arose from trying to be a one-man ministry, submitted to no one, answerable to no one." Charles paused to let his words soak in.

"Do you men realize that every one of us is just as exposed as Frank? Whom are we responsible to? To whom do we give an accounting? Haven't we all been like a bunch of spiritual Lone Rangers? Traveling all over the country as religious experts? Subject to deceptions and temptations far greater than any we ever knew simply as pastors?"

With tears in his eyes Charles leaned forward. "I want you all to know that I've been close to going over the edge like Frank. Only by the grace of God have I been spared; not because I'm better than he is. Through his problem I believe God is showing us how vulnerable we all are."

Conviction settled over us as Charles spoke. We looked at one another for a long minute, then each in turn confessed the same fears and temptations. Buffeted by long and exhausting hours of ministry, living apart from our families for days or weeks at a time, often flattered and fawned over by people grateful for the help they received—help which came from God and not from us—not a one of us could take credit for being spared the tragedy which had overtaken Frank.

"It's the spiritual warfare we're in," Derek said. "The devil's tactics are always to pick us off one by one. He waits for the right moment, then strikes at the weakest point in our defenses. Do you realize how many men with ministries of real power have disappeared from the Christian scene in the past few years?" And he listed several names familiar to us all; prominent ministries wrecked by greed, immorality, or some other lure of Satan.

"It seems to me," Derek continued, "that in every case these men made one fatal mistake: they failed to submit themselves to the Body of Christ. They all tried to go it alone!"

Bob Mumford broke in. "Perhaps God is showing us right here, not only the danger but the answer. For years I've longed to join my ministry to those of other men I could trust. I've come to know you three. I've seen the fruits of your ministries all across this nation. I'd like to be a part of what God is doing in and through each of you."

Bob had voiced the heartfelt desire of each of us. We suddenly knew the Holy Spirit had brought us together in that hotel room, not merely to pray for a beloved brother but to show us His sovereign intent to join our ministries together—and that meant submitting to one another as well as to Him.

There followed some of the most moving moments of my life as each of us placed himself and his ministry under the authority of the other three, pledging to support, encourage, correct, and pray for one another as men brought together in common service. In the time of worship and thanksgiving which followed, the Love of Christ seemed to fill the room until we could scarcely support the joy and the glory and the fullness that radiated there. Whatever of dark or evil we might encounter in the future, we had seen Jesus—and He was infinitely greater.

Over the next few days, as we met to explore the implications of united ministry, we came to marvel even more at God's economy. We discovered that each of us had areas of spiritual competence which others did not have, and that by ministering together, we could present "a whole Christ" and a "whole gospel" in a way none of us could alone. Not that our individual ministries would be completely submerged or abandoned, but that increasingly we would see them as only part of a much larger picture.

"It's like the medical profession," Bob Mumford reminded us. "Doctors in group practice can meet far more of the needs of their patients than even the best general practitioner. I don't have to be a specialist in deliverance because Don and Derek have been called into that field. I can depend on them in that area while I teach on subjects where I feel God has given me special insight."

"And, Bob, I don't have to be an expert in your field, or in Charles'," I added. "I've always felt Charles had a special grasp on Bible principles of divine authority and government. When I'm teaching in a city and find a need in that area, I can share—as a 'general practitioner'—what I know, while at the same time encouraging the people to call in a 'specialist,' to have Charles come and minister to them."

"Or better yet," Charles suggested, "we can go to that city together and share *as a team* the ministries God has given us. More than ever I've come to see why Jesus never sent out His disciples singly, but two by two, or in groups. He knew the kind of need they'd be encountering."

He knew the need. . . . There was a gray and drizzling rain as I climbed aboard a plane for Chicago a few days later. But the weather could not dampen my spirits. The lonely journey was over. Though I was keeping this appointment alone, the prayer and commitment of the others went with me.

The jet engines whined into life. As the huge craft lumbered to the end of the taxi strip and gently nosed around into position for takeoff, I had a brief glimpse down the length of the runway. Halfway down the field it disappeared into a wall of rain and mist.

Just like the life of faith, I thought. You can't see the end from the beginning.

The giant engines surged and the plane moved down the runway gaining speed. With a final thump of the landing gear we were free of the ground and climbing. Climbing swiftly through an overcast so thick I could barely see the end of the wing. As I glanced out the window I recalled the flight months earlier when fear had tormented me with thoughts of disaster. How long that had been the story of my life! Trying to move in faith, yet surrounded by fear.

But no more.

Of course tests and trials lay ahead in plenty—these are the way-stations of every Christian's journey. But not fear. And not isolation. These are no part of the Christian's luggage. By God's grace they were no longer part of mine. With joy I picked up the bundle He had marked for me: to proclaim the truth that Jesus came "to set the captives free."

Appendix A

Pages From My Notebook

WHILE I found no neat package of Bible teaching on the subject of Satan, with the use of concordances and commentaries and allowing for varying opinions and interpretations of Scripture, I came to see this picture of Satan and his hierarchy. (All quotes RSV, italics mine.)

THE REBELLION OF SATAN

The rebellion against God began in heaven. Satan, originally known as Lucifer, is believed by many Bible scholars to have been one of the three principal subrulers or archangels in heaven. These three (the other two are Michael and Gabriel), under God, ruled the lesser ranks and suborders of heavenly beings. All of them were created by God, through Jesus Christ.

He [Jesus Christ] is the image of the invisible God, the first-born of all Creation; for *in Him all things were created,* in heaven and on earth, visible and invisible, whether thrones or dominions or principalities or authorities—*all things were created through Him and for Him.* [Colossians 1:15, 16]

But the perfection of that initial divine order of creation was not destined to last. At some point before man inhabited the earth, Lucifer ("Light-bearer") rebelled against God, thus becoming Satan ("Adversary"). The reason for Lucifer's rebellion and subsequent downfall was pride. Five times in one brief passage, he exalts himself and his will against God and God's will.

How you are fallen from heaven, O Day Star [Lucifer] Son of Dawn! How you are cut down to the ground, you who laid the nations low! You said in your heart, "*I will* ascend to heaven; above the stars of God, *I will* set my throne on high; *I will* sit on the mount of assembly in the far north; *I will* ascend above the heights of the clouds, *I will* make myself like the Most High." But you are brought down to Sheol, to the depths of the Pit. [Isaiah 14:12–15]

Although neither the Scriptures nor biblical scholars attempt to pinpoint the time of the rebellion, whenever it took place, Jesus Christ, who "was in the beginning with God" (John 1:2), witnessed the fall.

And he said to them, "I saw Satan fall like lightning from heaven . . ." [Luke 10:18]

Because of his rebellion, Satan and his angels were cast out of heaven, and Satan set up his own rival kingdom in the "heavenly places" . . .

For we are not contending against flesh and blood, but against . . . spiritual hosts of wickedness in *the heavenly places*. [Ephesians 6:12]

or "midheaven" between the "third heaven" which is God's dwelling place and the visible heaven.

I know a man in Christ who fourteen years ago was caught up to *the third heaven* . . . into Paradise. [II Corinthians 12:2–3]

When God placed Adam and Eve in the Garden of Eden, Satan was on hand, in the form of a serpent, to do his lying work. The serpent is only one of many names given Satan in the Bible.

And the great dragon was thrown down, that ancient serpent, who is called the Devil and Satan . . . . [Revelation 12:9]

THE FALL OF MAN

God not only made Adam more like Himself than any other creature, but gave him Godlike authority over His entire creation on this planet.

Then God said, "Let us make man in our image, after our likeness; and let them have dominion . . . *over all the earth.*" [Genesis 1:26]

Satan tempted Eve and Adam to rebellion with the same motivation that caused his own fall: pride. "You shall be like God" (Genesis 3:5). When Adam and Eve succumbed to the temptation and disobeyed God, God's plan for man was disrupted. As a result of their disobedience, not only did they fall from their high estate, but the earth, too, which God had placed under man's rule, was corrupted.

And to Adam he said, "Because you have . . . eaten of the tree of which I commanded you, 'You shall not eat of it,' *cursed is the ground because of you* . . . ." [Genesis 3:17]

With the introduction of sin, decay and death became man's lot.

But of the tree of the knowledge of good and evil you shall not eat, for in the day that you eat of it you shall die. (Genesis 2:17)

Therefore as sin came into the world through one man, and death through sin, and so death spread to all men . . . . [Romans 5:12]

SATAN'S KINGDOM

When Adam hearkened to the devil in place of God, his fellowship with God was broken; his descendants became followers of Satan, "the sons of disobedience."

You once walked, following the course of this world, following the prince of the power of the air, the spirit that is now at work in the sons of disobedience . . . . [Ephesians 2:2]

In addition, man's God-given dominion over this planet likewise passed into Satan's control. Thus Satan could boast—when tempting Jesus—that all the kingdoms of the world belonged to him. Notice that while

He rejected the temptation, Jesus did not deny Satan's claim. Clearly, it was true. The word "delivered" can also be translated, "betrayed."

And the devil took him up, and showed him all the kingdoms of the world in a moment of time, and said to him, "To you I will give all this authority and their glory; for it has been delivered to me, and I give it to whom I will." [Luke 4:5–6]

The kingdoms of this world over which man was to have ruled were betrayed into the hands of Satan by man's disobedience, making Satan the "ruler" or god of this world.

. . . for the *ruler of this world* is coming. He has no power over me. [John 14:30]

. . . the god of this world has blinded the minds of the unbelievers . . . . [II Corinthians 4:4]

SATAN'S LEGIONS

But Satan does not carry on his devilish work singlehandedly. He is the ruler of a vast hierarchy which includes the angels who followed him in his rebellion (the third of the heavenly host who were under his command?).

Now war arose in heaven, Michael and his angels fighting against the dragon [Satan]; and the dragon and his angels fought . . . [Revelation 12:7]

This Satanic hierarchy is referred to in Scripture by such terms as "thrones," "dominions," "principalities," "authorities," and "powers."

He raised him from the dead and made him sit at his right hand in the heavenly places, far above all *rule and authority and power and dominion,* and above every name that is named, not only in this age, but also in that which is to come . . . . [Ephesians 1:20–21]

. . . that through the church the manifold wisdom of God might now be made known to *the principalities and powers* in the heavenly places. [Ephesians 3:10]

Put on the whole armor of God, that you may be able to stand against the wiles of the devil. For we are not contending against flesh and blood, but against the principalities, against the powers, against the world rulers of this present darkness, against the spiritual hosts of wickedness in the heavenly places. [Ephesians 6: 11–12]

When Paul speaks of "principalities and powers" it has been suggested he speaks of the higher ranks of the devil's angels, the "princes" which rule over great world areas such as those described in Daniel 10, where the "prince" of Persia and the "prince" of Greece battle the archangel Michael for twenty-one days to delay God's answer to Daniel's prayer.

The "world rulers of this present darkness" may correspond to those fallen angels who keep the world in darkness by hindering the bringing of the gospel of Jesus Christ.

Finally, the "spiritual hosts of wickedness in heavenly places" possibly indicate the lower order of angels and perhaps even the myriad of demon spirits which invade the earth and fill the atmosphere immediately surrounding it.

DEMONS

Angels are a heavenly order of being, created by God to be His messengers. Those that rebelled with Satan are, of course, "fallen angels" who do his bidding rather than God's.

Demon spirits appear to be of a different order of creation. Although some scholars are content to identify them as fallen angels, there are other theories. The historian Josephus spoke of demons as "the spirits of the wicked dead that enter into men that are alive," but there is nothing in the Scriptures which supports this view.

Some biblical scholars believe that demons are the disembodied spirits of a pre-Adamic race of beings, inhabitants of earth before God created Adam and Eve; beings who fell in league with or were corrupted by Satan and his angels when they were expelled from heaven. This theory would explain the propensity of the demons to seek embodiment in human—and even animal—form. They are driven to seek residence in some physical form, as Pember says in *Earth's Earliest Ages*, "by a longing to escape the intolerable condition of being unclothed."

Still other scholars propose the theory that demons are the spirits of the monstrous offspring of fallen angels and earth women. This occurrence is a theme in practically all ancient mythology and finds at least meager support from Scripture.

The sons of God saw that the daughters of men were fair; and they took to wife such of them as they chose. [Genesis 6:2]

These "sons of God" (presumably angels) were the same spiritual beings which presented themselves, along with Satan, before God in the book of Job.

Now there was a day when the sons of God came to present themselves before the Lord, and Satan also came among them. [Job 1:6]

An indication of rank even within this demonic realm is indicated by the two Greek words translated in English as "demon." One is *daimon,* and the other *daimonion,* the diminutive form of the word, signifying a demon of lesser power or authority. This distinction is further suggested by Jesus' words in Matthew.

Then he goes and brings with him *seven other spirits more evil than himself,* and they enter and dwell there; and the last state of that man becomes worse than the first. [Matthew 12:45]

THE WARFARE

According to Scripture, there exists an unrelenting spiritual warfare between the kingdom of God and the kingdom of Satan.

The reason the Son of God appeared was to destroy the works of the devil. [1 John 3:8]

God strives through the Body of Christ, the church, to restore fallen man to Himself . . .

He [God] has delivered us from the dominion of darkness and transferred us to the kingdom of his beloved son . . . [Colossians 1:13]

while Satan, God's arch-enemy, with his hosts, attempts to thwart God's purpose . . .

the god of this world has blinded the minds of the unbelievers. [II Corinthians 4:4]

The thief comes only to steal and kill and destroy . . . [John 10:10]

and to postpone his own final and inevitable destruction.

. . . for the devil has come down to you in great wrath, because he knows that his time is short. [Revelation 12:12]

And the devil . . . was thrown into the lake of fire and brimstone . . . and . . . will be tormented day and night for ever and ever. [Revelation 20:10]

The deliverance ministry—the authority given Christians over Satan and evil spirits in the name of the Lord Jesus Christ—provides one weapon in this cosmic struggle.

Appendix B

Where Deliverance
Is Ministered

AN INCREASING number of churches, fellowship groups, and individual Christians across the country include the ministry of deliverance as a part of their own well-balanced ministries of teaching, prayer, and personal counseling. A few are listed below. (Before contacting any such outside resource the individual is urged earnestly to endeavor to effect his own deliverance following the steps outlined in Chapter 17. Only if additional help still seems needed should the time and effort of these dedicated people be sought.)

Rev. H. A. Maxwell Whyte
United Apostolic Faith Church
2 Delbert Drive
Scarborough, Ontario
Canada

Al Allen
12 Wayland Street
North Cohocton, New York 14868

Mrs. Pat Brooks
New Testament Fellowship
Box 94
Ballston Lake, New York 12019

Schenectady Fullgospel Community
P.O. Box 1192
Scotia, New York 12302

Dr. Ed Atkinson
265 East Avenue
Greenville, Pennsylvania 16125

The Bair Foundation
565 W. Neshannock Avenue
New Wilmington,
Pennsylvania 16142

Rev. and Mrs. Luke Weaver
Grace Chapel
6530 Derry Street
Harrisburg, Pennsylvania

Mr. and Mrs. Hal Wallace
150 Jefferson Court
Staunton, Virginia

Dr. and Mrs. Robert Shumate
The Strait Gate
1715 Second Avenue
Columbus, Georgia 31903

Bayview Heights Baptist Church
850 Cottage Hill Avenue
Mobile, Alabama 36609

Rev. and Mrs. Dick Coleman
Westside Baptist Church
2508 Westside Drive
Leesburg, Florida 32748

Rev. Tom Hodgin
1325 N.E. 8th Avenue
Homestead, Florida 33010

Dr. J. Lawton Smith
9820 S.W. 62nd Court
Miami, Florida 33156

John Beckett
Dynamis
460 Avon-Belden Road
Avon Lake, Ohio 44012

Rev. Frank Longino
Valley Community Church
4413 East Pages Lane
Louisville, Kentucky 40272

Rev. Ernie Gruen
Full Faith Church of Love
2737 So. 42nd Street
Kansas City, Kansas 66106

Bill and Annette Mayne
Christian Faith Mission
805 West Missouri
Midland, Texas 79701

Rev. A. T. Ilseng, Jr.
New Testament Baptist Church
8314 Scyene Road
Dallas, Texas 75217

Rev. Wayne Butchart
22510 68th Place West
Mountlake Terrace,
Washington 98043

In addition to these in-person ministries, over sixty hours of Bible teaching by Don Basham, Derek Prince, Bob Mumford, and Charles Simpson have been recorded on television tape—including several hours on the deliverance ministry. These tapes are available for showing to groups and churches in your area. For information, contact Video Ministries, Inc., P.O. Box 22888, Fort Lauderdale, Florida 33315.